The Direction
of Poetry

THE
DIRECTION
OF POETRY

*An Anthology of Rhymed and
Metered Verse Written in
the English Language
Since 1975*

*Edited and
with an Introduction by*
Robert Richman

Houghton Mifflin Company
BOSTON
1988

Library of Congress Cataloging-in-Publication Data

The Direction of poetry.

1. American poetry— 20th century.
2. English poetry — 20th century.
3. English poetry — Commonwealth of Nations authors.
I. Richman, Robert, date.
PS615.D49   1988   811'.54'08   88–6772
ISBN 0–395–45426–3
ISBN 0–395–48355–7 (pbk.)

PRINTED IN THE UNITED STATES OF AMERICA

Q 10 9 8 7 6 5 4 3 2 1

Acknowledgments and copyright notices for individual poems begin on page 163.

EDITOR'S NOTE

This anthology contains the work of poets sharing a similar aesthetic perspective. It does not intend to be entirely representative of the times. It celebrates the work of a particular group of poets — the most important group to have emerged in the last fifteen years.

Contents

Introduction   xiii

FLEUR ADCOCK
   Future Work   1
   A Message   2
   Weathering   3
ELIZABETH BISHOP
   The Moose   3
   One Art   9
MICHAEL BLUMENTHAL
   Inventors   10
ALISON BRACKENBURY
   Whose Window?   11
   The Divers' Death   12
STANLEY BURNSHAW
   Talmudist   13
HENRI COLE
   The Prince Enters the Forest   13
HENRI COULETTE
   Postscript   14
   Correspondence   15
DONALD DAVIE
   Rousseau in His Day   15
   Ox-Bow   16
DICK DAVIS
   Childhood of a Spy   17
PETER DAVISON
   The Vanishing Point   17
   Questions of Swimming, 1935   19

CONTENTS

PETER KANE DUFAULT
A First Night   21
DOUGLAS DUNN
Elegy for the Lost Parish   22
War Blinded   23
CHARLES EDWARD EATON
The Lynx   24
DANIEL MARK EPSTEIN
From Homage to Mallarmé:
The Barrel Organ   25
Old Times   27
JAMES FENTON
God, A Poem   28
DAVID FERRY
Rereading Old Writing   29
Cythera   30
JOHN FULLER
Sonata   30
St. Sophia   32
REGINALD GIBBONS
Hoppy   33
DANA GIOIA
California Hills in August   34
The Next Poem   35
MELISSA GREEN
From The Squanicook Eclogues   36
MARILYN HACKER
Imaginary Translation   37
DONALD HALL
O Cheese   38
Granite and Grass   39
TONY HARRISON
Book Ends I   40
Confessional Poetry   41
The Queen's English   41
SEAMUS HEANEY
A Peacock's Feather   42
ANTHONY HECHT
The Deodand   44
The Ghost in the Martini   46

GEOFFREY HILL
Veni Coronaberis 50
From The Mystery of the Charity of Charles Péguy 50
From Hymns to Our Lady of Chartres 51

EDWARD HIRSCH
Fast Break 52

JOHN HOLLANDER
The Old Guitar 54

RICHARD HOWARD
From Ithaca: The Palace at Four A.M.:
Last Words 54

ANDREW HUDGINS
The Persistence of Nature in Our Lives 56

DONALD JUSTICE
Children Walking Home from School Through
Good Neighborhood 57
Psalm and Lament 58
In Memory of the Unknown Poet, Robert Boardman
Vaughn 60

X. J. KENNEDY
Hangover Mass 61
Terse Elegy for J. V. Cunningham 61

RICHARD KENNEY
La Brea 62

STANLEY KUNITZ
The Wellfleet Whale 63

BRAD LEITHAUSER
Angel 68
The Tigers of Nanzen-ji 69

WILLIAM LOGAN
Moorhen 71

DEREK MAHON
Table Talk 73
A Garage in Co. Cork 74

J. D. MCCLATCHY
At a Reading 76

JAMES MERRILL
Losing the Marbles 78

CONTENTS

JAMES MICHIE
  Nine Times   85
  Discoverer   85
RICHARD MOORE
  The Visitors   86
FREDERICK MORGAN
  February 11, 1977   87
HERBERT MORRIS
  The Road   88
HOWARD MOSS
  Morning Glory   90
ANDREW MOTION
  Writing   90
  These Days   91
PAUL MULDOON
  Why Brownlee Left   93
LES A. MURRAY
  The Widower in the Country   93
  Sydney and the Bush   94
HOWARD NEMEROV
  Insomnia I   95
  The Makers   96
  The War in the Air   97
JOHN FREDERICK NIMS
  Tide Turning   98
LESLIE NORRIS
  The Girls of Llanbadarn
    (from the Welsh of Dafydd ap Gwilym)   99
ROBERT PINSKY
  Ralegh's Prizes   101
KATHA POLLITT
  Of the Scythians   101
  Two Fish   102
CHRISTOPHER REID
  The Gardeners   103
MICHAEL J. ROSEN
  Total Eclipse   104
GIBBONS RUARK
  Larkin   105

CAROL RUMENS
 Vocation 106
 In the Cloud of Unknowing 107
MARY JO SALTER
 England 110
 Welcome to Hiroshima 110
GJERTRUD SCHNACKENBERG
 Supernatural Love 112
ALAN SHAPIRO
 Familiar Story 114
L. E. SISSMAN
 Cockaigne: A Dream 115
 December 27, 1966 117
C. H. SISSON
 Black Rocks 118
WILLIAM JAY SMITH
 Journey to the Interior 119
 Bachelor's-Buttons 120
W. D. SNODGRASS
 Mutability 121
ELIZABETH SPIRES
 Two Shadows 122
 0° 122
TIMOTHY STEELE
 The Sheets 123
 Aurora 124
ANNE STEVENSON
 The Price 125
 The Fiction-Makers 126
 Making Poetry 128
MAY SWENSON
 Morning at Point Dume 129
ANTHONY THWAITE
 Simple Poem 130
 Dream Time 130
CHARLES TOMLINSON
 Rhymes 131
 The Shaft 132

CONTENTS

DAVID WAGONER
My Father's Garden 133
On Motel Walls 134
JEFFREY WAINWRIGHT
The Fierce Dream 135
Illumination 136
DEREK WALCOTT
The Young Wife 136
ROBERT PENN WARREN
What Voice at Moth-Hour 138
History During Nocturnal Snowfall 138
Last Meeting 139
ROSANNA WARREN
History as Decoration 141
To Max Jacob 142
THEODORE WEISS
Another and Another and . . . 143
From Every Second Thought 144
RICHARD WILBUR
Lying 146
Transit 148
The Catch 149

Introduction

TO THE GENERAL READER, who has all but given up on contemporary poetry as a source of pleasure, this book will come as something of a surprise. After two decades of obscure, linguistically flat poetry, there has been a decisive shift. In both the United States and Britain, narration, characterization, and, perhaps most significantly, musicality are showing new vigor.

The return to musicality is tied to a recent upsurge among poets in the use of metrical language. I'll discuss in due course the specific uses to which meter is put by the poets here. One doesn't, in any case, need a technical knowledge of rhyme and meter to be able to admire the poetry in these pages. The sheer sensuous appeal of the verse can be appreciated even by those with a poetically "untrained" ear and eye. Few unspecialized readers will fail to be delighted by these lines from Anne Stevenson's "Making Poetry":

> "You have to inhabit poetry
> if you want to make it."
>
> And what's "to inhabit"?
>
> To be in the habit of, to wear
> words, sitting in the plainest light,
> in the silk of morning, in the shoe of night;
> a feeling, bare and frondish in surprising air;
> familiar . . . rare.

as they will by these, from Derek Walcott's "The Young Wife":

Ah, but the mirror — the mirror
which you believe has seen
the traitor you feel you are —
clouds, though you wipe it clean!

or these, from Timothy Steele's "Aurora":

Your sleep is so profound
This room seems a recess
Awaiting consciousness.
Gauze curtains, drawn around
The postered bed, confute
Each waking attribute —
Volition, movement, sound.

Just as pleasure-giving is the imagery of the poems in this book. One of the more vivid images is Gjertrud Schnackenberg's depiction, in "Supernatural Love," of a young girl watching, through the eye of a needle, her father at a dictionary stand. Another is Mary Jo Salter's image of a billboard in Hiroshima, "brought to you in living English / by Toshiba Electric." And then there is J. D. McClatchy's unforgettable picture — in "At a Reading" — of a deaf woman having the recited poem helped "out of its disguise of words" by an interpreter using sign language. McClatchy's poem is about the way poetry re-creates emotions in the reader, how verse forges a bond between poet and reader through the abstract medium of words. It is about, that is, the experience of everyone who reads this book.

Melodious language and vibrant imagery are not the only means these poets have of capturing the reader's attention. The characters — some invented, some not — in certain poems are equally engrossing. In Robert Penn Warren's "Last Meeting," the narrator and the woman he encounters are the kind of fully realized characters one meets in the best prose fiction. The same is true of the speaker in Andrew Motion's "Writing." This poem, narrated by a writer (whose own writing appears in the poem in italics), deals with the travails of finding one's voice after, as the writer-narrator puts it, "what felt like a lifetime of rent." But "Last Meeting" and "Writing" not only contain fascinating characters; they are rich in dramatic effect as well. Another poem brimming with drama is Herbert Morris's "The Road."

The truth is, there is a whole range of emotion and experience rendered marvelously in this book. From the great good humor of Fleur Adcock's "Future Work," to the touching meditation on the gulf between lovers in Elizabeth Spires's "Shadow to Shadow"; from Derek Mahon's mundane ode to his writing table ("Table Talk"), to Geoffrey Hill's visionary leap into the unknown (in the poem from "Hymns to Our Lady of Chartres") — the poetry here is extremely appealing and accessible, and hardly the remote and unfamiliar territory contemporary verse has long been perceived to be.

However diverse the themes or emotions used by these poets, though, all are united in their use of metered language. This is the principal feature of the poetry here, and the central trait of the "movement" being surveyed in this book. Not since the late forties and fifties have so many poets on both sides of the Atlantic made meter so integral a part of their poetic vision. And not since the fifties has such a large number of the most gifted younger poets chosen to make the mastery of metrical form a test of their achievement. Among other things, the publication of this anthology invalidates the countless critical judgments, expressed in the sixties and seventies, of the death of metrical verse.

Thirty years ago it would have seemed strange to define formal poetry as verse written in metrical feet. If this book were being assembled then, it would have been sufficient to say that it contained sonnets, villanelles, heroic couplets, and so on. Such a description is no longer adequate. The free verse orthodoxy that has reigned for the last twenty-five years in the United States and Great Britain has insinuated itself so deeply into our respective poetic cultures that the entire conception of form has been corrupted. The last two decades have seen a plethora of free verse "sestinas," "pantoums," and "sonnets." Perhaps the most influential examples of free verse "sonnets" were those written by Robert Lowell which appeared in the volumes entitled *Notebook* (1970), *For Lizzie and Harriet* (1973), *The Dolphin* (1973), and *Day by Day* (1977). Rhyme has often been used in conjunction with free verse during this period as well, as have stanza forms such as quatrains, quintets, tercets, and couplets. John Ashbery's "Some Trees" is an outstanding example of unmetrical couplets. A recent anthology entitled *Strong Measures: Contemporary American Poetry in Traditional Forms*, edited by Philip Dacey and David Jauss, provides a showcase for precisely this kind of hybrid verse, in which the pretense of a traditional form is used without employing any of its technical attributes.

The consistent use of a metrical foot, then, unites the poets in this anthology. A metrical foot consists of one, two, or three syllables, only one of which is stressed; and these syllables are grouped in lines of a (usually) fixed number of feet. The use of this foot guarantees the repetition of a stress at established intervals, giving each line of verse a series of expected climactic accents. These accents, or stresses, may be grouped closely together or stretched out in a line, but never protracted to the extent that they dissipate the pattern of anticipation the poet sets up.*

Stress and syllable-stress verse are therefore the dominant metrical forms the reader will encounter in these pages. I have not attempted to represent as many different forms as possible. Literary quality was the primary criterion for inclusion, and it was inevitable that certain verse forms would be omitted. This selection includes sonnets (by Alison Brackenbury, Tony Harrison, and Marilyn Hacker), villanelles (by Elizabeth Bishop, Donald Justice, and Henri Coulette), blank verse (by L. E. Sissman, Peter Davison, and Geoffrey Hill), rhyming quatrains (by Dick Davis, Douglas Dunn, Anthony

---

* The permissible substitutions for an iambic foot proposed by George Saintsbury in *Historical Manual of English Prosody* (1910) still apply to poets writing in meter today: the trochee (/-), anapest (--/), spondee (//), and, less frequently, dactyl (/--) and pyrrhic (--). Saintsbury's *Historical Manual* is a compressed edition of his three-volume *History of English Prosody*, which was completed in 1910.

Hecht, and Robert Penn Warren), sapphic stanzas (by Timothy Steele), heroic couplets (by X. J. Kennedy), tercets (by Fleur Adcock and Charles Edward Eaton), triplets (by Gjertrud Schnackenberg), a sestina (by John Frederick Nims), and a handful of others. But just as many metrical verse forms are absent. I ruled out most quantitative syllabic poetry on the grounds that it has no regular pattern of stresses. The syllabic poems that have been included — Richard Wilbur's "The Catch," Brad Leithauser's "The Tigers of Nanzen-ji," Reginald Gibbons's "Hoppy," and Richard Moore's "The Visitors" — are all enlivened by the addition of stress and rhyme patterns.

There are certain younger poets whom one thinks of with respect and admiration when compiling a book consisting of poems written in a formal metric — W. S. Di Piero and Norman Williams, to name just two. But since such poets have an ambivalent attitude toward meter, moving in and out of it in their poems, they have been excluded. Their work falls outside the scope of this particular anthology.

The omission of Amy Clampitt should also be mentioned. Many readers view Clampitt as a formalist poet. In truth, Clampitt seldom writes metrically. Just as problematic, however, is the conflation in many of her poems of "high" poetic language and a kind of surrealism that was popular in the sixties and seventies. The result — in my view, at any rate — is an unlikely and finally unsatisfying juxtaposition of the poetic spirits of Marianne Moore and John Ashbery.

The rehabilitation of a certain technical discipline should never be undertaken because it is deemed to be sufficient in itself. The poets in these pages all use meter because it allows them to probe deeper into the experience or emotion they are exploring in their poems. The use to which meter is put, however, varies considerably. In some poems, the beat of the meter functions as a musical analogue to the emotion the poet is conveying. In Donald Hall's "O Cheese," for example, the headlong rush of strong stresses lends his celebration of one of the basic verities of life an enhancing pulse. Similarly, the metric of Brad Leithauser's "The Tigers of Nanzen-ji" offers euphonic affirmation of the poet's discovery that there is nothing to fear in the world of artful appearances. And in Geoffrey Hill's long poem "The Mystery of the Charity of Charles Péguy," which is excerpted here, the moral ambiguity of the poet's role as historical witness is reflected in the "unresolved" rough pentameter and half rhymes.

Often, specific variations within the iambic line respond to the perceptual or emotional twists of the poem. In Richard Wilbur's "Transit," for instance, the first eight lines of iambic pentameter (a metric corresponding to *today today today today today*) contain trochaic substitutions (/ -) in the first foot of the second and seventh lines. The substitutions given these lines an appropriate jolt.

> A woman I have never seen before
> Steps from the darkness of her town-house door
> At just that crux of time when she is made
> So beautiful that she or time must fade.
>
> What use to claim that as she tugs her gloves
> A phantom heraldry of all the loves
> Blares from the lintel? That the staggered sun
> Forgets, in his confusion, how to run?

Similarly, Andrew Hudgins's "The Persistence of Nature in Our Lives" starts with a series of five routine iambic tetrameter lines (except for the slightly varied second line, which contains nine syllables). These lines are followed by one that reads:

> the persistence of nature in our lives

The switch to ten syllables, the first six of which are given over to two anapestic feet (- - /, - - /), stretches out and slows down the line — a perfect means of fortifying the impression of nature's obstinacy. But in the nonsense verse of James Fenton, X. J. Kennedy, and William Jay Smith, the more or less unvaried metronomic regularity of the beat is a fitting accompaniment to the delightful, but simple, silliness of the sentiment.

In some poems, meter functions usefully as a metaphor. In Wilbur's "Transit," the metrical foundation serves as a kind of launching pad for the spiritually transcendent flash the poem depicts. In this poem, as in others, meter represents the rational, orderly life that, for all its apparent mundanity, contains within it the possibility of release from what Brad Leithauser calls, in a poem not included here, "the straightening domain of the plausible." Meter is used to this end in "Total Eclipse" by Michael J. Rosen. Here, the miraculous coincidence of the eclipse (an alignment involving not just moon, earth, and sun but the two lovers in the poem as well) is the "one held moment" that exceeds the ordinary. In Stanley Kunitz's "The Wellfleet Whale," however, the metrical footing is not something to be outstripped but to fall back on—a rhythmic consolation for the loss of awe and wonder in our time that is the poet's central theme.

In other poems, rhyme and meter challenge the emotion or perception expressed in the poem. This generates a tension appropriate to the poet's aims. In Tony Harrison's sonnets, for example, rhyme and meter are brought to bear on the dialect of working-class England. And what an unlikely coalition it is! Harrison's poems are linguistic battlegrounds on which we see vividly enacted the struggle between the demands of the cultural past, represented by form, and the demands of the present, represented by the idiom of Leeds (Harrison's place of birth). The effect is metrical variation and substitution aplenty:

> But your father was a simple working man,
> they'll say, and didn't speak in those full rhymes.
> His words when they came would scarcely scan.
>
> Mi dad's did scan, like yours do, many times!

The conflict between inherited formal measures and contemporary colloquial idioms is at the heart of the poetry of L. E. Sissman as well. Like Harrison, Sissman sets for himself the imposing task of bringing the grace and artistry of formal metrics not only to the dialects of his particular social milieu but to every mundane aspect of the middle-class life he knew so well. Sissman's fusing of meter with the most quotidian and unheroic cause of death our deeply quotidian and unheroic century can offer—cancer— has resulted in one of the greatest, one might even say heroic, achievements in blank verse in our time. Indeed, Sissman's achievement in this form is rivaled only by that of Philip Larkin.*

Anthony Hecht grapples with a related issue in his poems: the way rhyme and meter tend to cloak or prettify the anguish to which the poet often directs his attention. To swathe "in exotic finery, in loose silks," as Hecht writes in "The Deodand," the misery of the past (or, in the case of "The Ghost in the Martini," the speaker's personal suffering) is morally suspect, or so Hecht thinks. The consequence, at any rate, is that every sweet rhyme and every satisfying beat reminds us paradoxically of the *cost* of our indulgence in their beauty. Rosanna Warren is also troubled by the way artistry conceals suffering. When she argues, in "History as Decoration," that "We pay for beauty; beautiful / are gorgeous crimes we cannot feel," the judgment extends to her own "gorgeous crime" of poetry. The poem reflects her dilemma with a jagged metric.

Rhyme is used just as scrupulously by these poets. Elizabeth Bishop's meditation, in "One Art," on the ease with which we lose—the way we go about "losing farther, losing faster," as she puts it—is animated by the cascade of rhymes in the villanelle form she adopts. And in Gjertrud Schnackenberg's "Supernatural Love," the three-way bond among child, father, and "Christ's flowers" is reinforced by means of the insistent *a a a* rhyme scheme. The poem suggests that the girl's emotional connection with her

---

* Farrar, Straus and Giroux, Larkin's American publisher, refused to grant permission to use three of Larkin's uncollected poems in this anthology. This is unfortunate, as Larkin's last poems were to be given a central place in both the introduction and text of *The Direction of Poetry*.

father will elevate her in the same fashion words are elevated through the magical linkage of rhyme.

There can be little doubt, then, that the freshness of the poetry here owes much to its reliance on metrical language. But as important as meter is to these poets, it is only one aspect of their work. Meter may be a powerful and effective means to an end, as these poets believe it to be, but it is not an end in itself. If meter continues to prove to be such a flexible and rewarding accompaniment to the idioms, perceptions, and emotions of our time, the chances are good that it will thrive well into the next century. Whatever it may portend for the future, however, it is clearly the best means for poets to come to terms with their experiences now.

ROBERT RICHMAN

The Direction
of Poetry

Fleur Adcock

 FUTURE WORK

"Please send future work"
  — *Editor's note on a rejection slip*

It is going to be a splendid summer.
The apple tree will be thick with golden russets
expanding weightily in the soft air.
I shall finish the brick wall beside the terrace
and plant out all the geranium cuttings.
Pinks and carnations will be everywhere.

She will come out to me in the garden,
her bare feet pale on the cut grass,
bringing jasmine tea and strawberries on a tray.
I shall be correcting the proofs of my novel
(third in a trilogy — simultaneous publication
in four continents); and my latest play

will be in production at the Aldwych
starring Glenda Jackson and Paul Scofield
with Olivier brilliant in a minor part.
I shall probably have finished my translations
of Persian creation myths and the Pre-Socratics
(drawing new parallels) and be ready to start

on Lucretius. But first I'll take a break
at the chess championships in Manila —
on present form, I'm fairly likely to win.
And poems? Yes, there will certainly be poems:
they sing in my head, they tingle along my nerves.
It is all magnificently about to begin.

 A MESSAGE

Discreet, not cryptic. I write to you from the garden
in tawny, provoking August; summer is just
on the turn. The lawn is hayseeds and grassy dust.

There are brilliant yellow daisies, though, and fuchsia
(you'll know why) and that mauve and silvery-grey
creeper under the apple tree where we lay.

There have been storms. The apples are few, but heavy,
heavy. And where blossom was, the tree
surges with bright pink flowers — the sweet pea

has taken it over again. Things operate
oddly here. Remember how I found
the buddleia dead, and cut it back to the ground?

That was in April. Now it's ten feet high:
thick straight branches — they've never been so strong —
leaves like a new species, half a yard long,

and spikes of flowers, airily late for their season
but gigantic. A mutation, is it? Well,
summers to come will test it. Let time tell.

Gardens are rife with sermon-fodder. I delve
among blossoming accidents for their designs
but make no statement. Read between these lines.

 WEATHERING

Literally thin-skinned, I suppose, my face
catches the wind off the snow-line and flushes
with a flush that will never wholly settle. Well:
that was a metropolitan vanity,
wanting to look young for ever, to pass.

I was never a pre-Raphaelite beauty,
nor anything but pretty enough to satisfy
men who need to be seen with passable women.
But now that I am in love with a place
which doesn't care how I look, or if I'm happy,

happy is how I look, and that's all.
My hair will turn grey in any case,
my nails chip and flake, my waist thicken,
and the years work all their usual changes.
If my face is to be weather-beaten as well

that's little enough lost, a fair bargain
for a year among lakes and fells, when simply
to look out of my window at the high pass
makes me indifferent to mirrors and to what
my soul may wear over its new complexion.

Elizabeth Bishop

 THE MOOSE

> *For Grace Bulmer Bowers*

From narrow provinces
of fish and bread and tea,

home of the long tides
where the bay leaves the sea
twice a day and takes
the herrings long rides,

where if the river
enters or retreats
in a wall of brown foam
depends on if it meets
the bay coming in,
the bay not at home;

where, silted red,
sometimes the sun sets
facing a red sea,
and others, veins the flats'
lavender, rich mud
in burning rivulets;

on red, gravelly roads,
down rows of sugar maples,
past clapboard farmhouses
and neat, clapboard churches,
bleached, ridged as clamshells,
past twin silver birches,

through late afternoon
a bus journeys west,
the windshield flashing pink,
pink glancing off of metal,
brushing the dented flank
of blue, beat-up enamel;

down hollows, up rises,
and waits, patient, while
a lone traveller gives

kisses and embraces
to seven relatives
and a collie supervises.

Goodbye to the elms,
to the farm, to the dog.
The bus starts. The light
grows richer; the fog,
shifting, salty, thin,
comes closing in.

Its cold, round crystals
form and slide and settle
in the white hens' feathers,
in gray glazed cabbages,
on the cabbage roses
and lupins like apostles;

the sweet peas cling
to their wet white string
on the whitewashed fences;
bumblebees creep
inside the foxgloves,
and evening commences.

One stop at Bass River.
Then the Economies —
Lower, Middle, Upper;
Five Islands, Five Houses,
where a woman shakes a tablecloth
out after supper.

A pale flickering. Gone.
The Tantramar marshes
and the smell of salt hay.
An iron bridge trembles

and a loose plank rattles
but doesn't give way.

On the left, a red light
swims through the dark:
a ship's port lantern.
Two rubber boots show,
illuminated, solemn.
A dog gives one bark.

A woman climbs in
with two market bags,
brisk, freckled, elderly.
"A grand night. Yes, sir,
all the way to Boston."
She regards us amicably.

Moonlight as we enter
the New Brunswick woods,
hairy, scratchy, splintery;
moonlight and mist
caught in them like lamb's wool
on bushes in a pasture.

The passengers lie back.
Snores. Some long sighs.
A dreamy divagation
begins in the night,
a gentle, auditory,
slow hallucination. . . .

In the creakings and noises,
an old conversation
— not concerning us,
but recognizable, somewhere,
back in the bus:
Grandparents' voices

uninterruptedly
talking, in Eternity:
names being mentioned,
things cleared up finally;
what he said, what she said,
who got pensioned;

deaths, deaths and sicknesses;
the year he remarried;
the year (something) happened.
She died in childbirth.
That was the son lost
when the schooner foundered.

He took to drink. Yes.
She went to the bad.
When Amos began to pray
even in the store and
finally the family had
to put him away.

"Yes . . ." that peculiar
affirmative. "Yes . . ."
A sharp, indrawn breath,
half groan, half acceptance,
that means "Life's like that.
We know it (also death)."

Talking the way they talked
in the old featherbed,
peacefully, on and on,
dim lamplight in the hall,
down in the kitchen, the dog
tucked in her shawl.

Now, it's all right now
even to fall asleep

just as on all those nights.
— Suddenly the bus driver
stops with a jolt,
turns off his lights.

A moose has come out of
the impenetrable wood
and stands there, looms, rather,
in the middle of the road.
It approaches; it sniffs at
the bus's hot hood.

Towering, antlerless,
high as a church,
homely as a house
(or, safe as houses).
A man's voice assures us
"Perfectly harmless. . . ."

Some of the passengers
exclaim in whispers,
childishly, softly,
"Sure are big creatures."
"It's awful plain."
"Look! It's a she!"

Taking her time,
she looks the bus over,
grand, otherworldly.
Why, why do we feel
(we all feel) this sweet
sensation of joy?

"Curious creatures,"
says our quiet driver,
rolling his *r*'s.

"Look at that, would you."
Then he shifts gears.
For a moment longer,

by craning backward,
the moose can be seen
on the moonlit macadam;
then there's a dim
smell of moose, an acrid
smell of gasoline.

 ONE ART

The art of losing isn't hard to master;
so many things seem filled with the intent
to be lost that their loss is no disaster.

Lose something every day. Accept the fluster
of lost door keys, the hour badly spent.
The art of losing isn't hard to master.

Then practice losing farther, losing faster:
places, and names, and where it was you meant
to travel. None of these will bring disaster.

I lost my mother's watch. And look! my last, or
next-to-last, of three loved houses went.
The art of losing isn't hard to master.

I lost two cities, lovely ones. And, vaster,
some realms I owned, two rivers, a continent.
I miss them, but it wasn't a disaster.

— Even losing you (the joking voice, a gesture
I love) I shan't have lied. It's evident

the art of losing's not too hard to master
though it may look like (*Write* it!) like disaster.

Michael Blumenthal

 INVENTORS

> Imagine being the first to say: *surveillance.* . . .
> — *Howard Nemerov*

"Imagine being the first to say: *surveillance*,"
the mouth taking in air like a swimmer, the tongue
light as an astronaut, gliding across the roof
of the mouth, the eyes burning like the eyes of Fleming
looking at mold and thinking: *penicillin.*

Imagine Franklin holding his key that dark night,
the clouds rolling across the sky's roof
like a poet's tongue, the air heavy with some
unnamed potential, the whole thing suspended
from a string like a vocal cord waiting to say:
electricity.

Or imagine digging for shale in some dull Oklahoma,
how the ground is a parched throat waiting for moisture,
and you all derricky and impatient, knowing something
you have yet no name for might rise and surprise you.
Imagine being the first to say: *petroleum.*

Some night, dry as an old well and speechless
beneath a brilliant moon, think of Heisenberg
taking his ruler to the world for a measure
and finding, in the measuring, an irrevocable changing.

Imagine being the first to say, with confidence:
uncertainty.

It goes on like this always. A poet stops in the woods
to clear his throat, and out comes: *convolvulus*.
A biologist rolls over during the night to hold
her husband, thinking: *peristalsis*. A choreographer
watches the sunrise over Harlem, whispering: *tour-jeté,
ronde-de-jambe*.

Just think of it —
your tongue rolling over the first *pharmacopoeia*
like a new lover, the shuddering thrill of it,
the way the air parts in front of your mouth, widening
the world in its constant uncertainty. Go on.
Let your mind wander. Imagine being the first to say:
I love you, oregano, onomatopoeia.

Just imagine it.

Alison Brackenbury

 WHOSE WINDOW?

Whose window are you gazing through,
Whose face is stilled between your hands?
The glass glows deeper than your eyes
Where quick lights sink: as feet through sands.

Into your darkness first snow drives,
No soft meander, aimless drift,
But straight as water. Crumbling bright,
Sharp crystals flash, as if they lived.

Now when the great wind throbs the door
When street-light and small hedge are drowned
My face turns open into night.
I am not safe. No, I am found
Melting the hard bolts back. The hall
Is filled with dark air, ice-clouds blow:

A warm face sleeps. I am the snow,
Uncatch your window. Let me through.

 THE DIVERS' DEATH

The two dead divers hauled up in their bell
Died not from lack of air, but the great cold,
The linking cable severed and they fell
Fathoms of dark, away from tides that rolled,
From gulls that rode the storm, from sun that warmed
Down where the wind dropped; and the hands that cried,
Used to much, not this. No breath
Deserved the line to break, the spasm, black to death.

And so the dead child, taken quickly out
from white walls, the emptied woman. Or
brain-damaged babies, who can roll about
like small sea-creatures on the padded floor.
Someone washes them and listens for
their cries; they turned their heads when we went near.
But someone might have wished for them a knife
to exorcise the darkness of that life.

Deeper than the fast, bright fishes go
are the great depths that divers cannot kill —
what knife could cut so bitterly? And so
We are love's strange seabirds. We dive there, still.

Stanley Burnshaw

 TALMUDIST

Gloat, glittering talmudist,
With your eastern eye, your northern eye, your western eye;
The days are a fog of clashing words: cleave
If you can — warp with your buzz-saw brain a light-filled
Path shallow enough for a heart to follow!

Why do you fist your words
With your merchant's hand, your scholar's hand, your toiler's
    hand?
Is a god you smother the dynamo of your fury
Or a wraith you reasoned into existence in hope
It would pierce your eye with joys? Or a heartsick need

For a heaven-on-earth perfection
That drives you, though you have found there can be no
    right
Unmixed with wrong. Where will you go when the moment
Strikes and your arms, defying brain, reach out
To your brothers' will, your homeland's will, your body's
    will?

Henri Cole

 THE PRINCE ENTERS THE FOREST

full of courage and promise like the geese gone away,
his horse trembling beneath him on the trail of burr.

He cannot, despite all that he will spare her,
bring his thoughts from her continuous sleep, so he prays,

now and again embarrassed by her,
imagining her dress half opened from decay,
the coat of dust at her lips — which will he touch first? —
her sewing hand fallen like a bird from its cage,

the red bead still fluttering on its bill.
Will he kiss her lids or raise them
and touch each astonished iris, shrunken and still?
Will she sleep on and on in her kingdom of thorn,

or will the world catch in her heart, in his mouth,
and rage like the geese overhead, warring south?

Henri Coulette

 POSTSCRIPT

There are some questions one should know by heart.
A world without them must be shadowless.
Who was it said, Come let us kiss and part?

The one who asked, Why is this apple tart?
And dreamed the serpent was the letter S?
There are some questions one should know by heart.

It was the thorn that plotted to outsmart
The cunning of the rose with such success.
Who was it said, Come let us kiss and part?

There are interiors none may map or chart:
In your voice, crying, was a wilderness.
There are some questions one should know by heart.

Your ape and echo from the bitter start,
This mirror mourns your image's caress.
Who was it said, Come let us kiss and part?

We had too little craft and too much art.
We thought two noes would make a perfect yes.
There are some questions one should know by heart.
Who was it said, Come let us kiss and part?

 CORRESPONDENCE

The letter lies unanswered, thus free of lies.
The light all day has travelled the crowded pages,
Shifting the shadows, changing the hue of ink.
The truths, if truths there are, are stationary.

Now night comes on, from your time zone to mine.
The moon is tentative, not wholly herself,
And the owl bells, and the owl's mate bells back,
A dialogue of sorts, question and answer,

The answer being but the question asked.
East of your sleep, deep in the zodiac,
Tomorrow is already chronicled.
Oh, I shall write you what you want to hear.

Donald Davie

 ROUSSEAU IN HIS DAY

So many nights the solitary lamp had burned;
So many nights his lone mind, slowing down
Deliberately, had questioned, as it turned

Mooning upon its drying stem, what arc
Over a lifetime day had moved him through.

Always he hoped he might deserve a Plutarch,
Not to be one posterity forgot.
Nor have we. He has left his mark: one tight
Inched-around circuit of the screw of light,
As glowing shadows track the life of roses
Over unchosen soil-crumbs. It was not
What he'd expected or the world supposes.

OX-BOW

The time is at an end.
   The river swirled
Into an ox-bow bend, but now
   It shudders and re-unites:
   Adversary! Friend!

Adverse currents drove
   This pair apart.
A twin tormented throe embraced,
   Enisled between them, one
   Quadrant of earth, one grove.

Now for each other they yearn
   Across the eyot
That the peculiar flow of each
   Carved out, determined. Now,
   Now to each other they turn,

And it is past belief
   That once they forked;
Or that, upstream and bypassed, trees
   Mirrored in mid-reach still
   Break into annual leaf.

Dick Davis

 CHILDHOOD OF A SPY

Much earlier than most he found
Most things are not as they appear;
The mousy child who makes no sound
Lives in a haze of smothered fear —

Where is he safe? Reality
Is something glimpsed through misted glass;
A closed, adult conspiracy,
A frontier post he may not pass.

Truth is a secret and he learns
Its lonely code; the bit lip trembles
But says nothing — compassion turns
To hatred that a smile dissembles.

The frontier will be down, his fear
A state ubiquitous as air;
And, vindicated, he will hear
Their cry of candour and despair.

Peter Davison

 THE VANISHING POINT

New Year's Day 1984

Snow crept up overnight as we slept
and powdered the surface of the earth so lightly
the footpaths stirred, as smooth as dusted skin.

An uncut beard of grass darkened the field.
I had awakened to the shimmering landscape
from a sleep sunk in sullen dreams, entombed
in the companionship of friends long dead
who accelerated along gravel country roads
or city streets crammed with traffic
toward no end anyone would have wanted to reach.
Their destination was a point deeper than ever
in the closed and unforgiving past
where love enacts its remorseless guzzling.

This morning, though, was dusted with the present
as though brushed by the smoky fragrance
of sleep. It held there for the moment.
No wind stirred up the snow along the branches,
no wheel crushed down a snowflake on the road.
This present moment, exquisitely poised,
had not yet given in to the scramble of time
but seemed to hold itself back from moving on
out of a night which hurtled in drunken zigzags
through one of the dreams where we are never alone.
Carried by trains, motorcycles, elevators,
we are always passengers, always companioned,
sniffing out the smelly trails of childhood,
flaunting a thousand newly-sewn disguises.
Where those dreams take us, no matter how eager
their search, they never end in arrival.

Now the present is inching toward the future.
At the silent feeding station chickadees chirp.
Over the marsh black air flourishes flecks
of irregular white, more snowflakes, *storme still*.
The sky as it unbends relents a little
and grows lighter. A dog barks in protest
at the iron day, indignant at its silence.
The perfection of this morning hour has yielded,
without anticipation, to the fact

that time is coasting forward, turning momentum
into the new year's elliptical glide.

Poised on the incoming day, between tides
of sleep and waking, I ride on the waters of time,
whose movement, steady as the orb of earth,
makes only one general statement: *Change is all.*
The weather system, the troubling dreams of travel,
a scrap of geography discarded here
in the glacial scree of leftover landscape —
these happenings seek no end, no destination.
Each moment wishes us to move farther on
into a sequence we can follow at most
to vanishing point. We can see no farther,
though time seems to pause and wait for us at times
and measure us and move along again.

 QUESTIONS OF SWIMMING, 1935

For Robert Penn Warren

What was the nub of wonder? Was it
the man, giant to my child-eyes, strapping
a shiny black rubber bathing cap over the cap
of his red hair, plugging his nostrils and ears,
and lowering his lean body into the yellow
lake in Colorado, down into the frightening
water, to begin the steady trudgen
that took him, as long as my skipping patience
could endure, steadily farther from sight
as far as the far shore, a mile, and without
pause, brought him back to me, bobbing
far out in the water, then thrashing,
then finally splashing, and gasping and rising,
and then, again, human and near me, dripping and walking?

Wonder at the man, or at the task?
What sort of way was it to spend
an hour in thrashing straight across a lake
and, turning, swimming straight back to the start?
Where was he setting out for when he began, fresh?
Where had he been to when he returned, winded?

Or take the style: laboring akimbo,
a steady crawl across the sheet of water
without a pause to whoop or whistle or blow,
a style as awkward as inexorable,
in which the completion of the task seemed to count
more to the swimmer than not drowning.

The lake? A captive body
the dry climate had permitted
to rest between the knees
Boulder had bulldozed to keep
the water from evaporating: a reservoir.
The man swam back and forth between its walls.

What of the rhythm of the exercise?
Not like a dog or deer that simply walks
on water, but a dactyl, a quantitative
excursus, a distribution of forces between
the limbs, these legs working like scissors,
these arms working like flails, these lungs
working like bellows, this mind working,
working on lessened oxygen, this body
moving against every interference to imitate
its forgotten grandfather, the fish.

To the destructive element submit yourself,
and with the exertions of your hands and feet
make the deep, deep sea keep you up.
Once kept up, where do we go from there?

To the headwaters, the spawning ground?
To the floating pyre, the fire ship?
To the other shore? Which is the other shore?
Could it be the place where a boy could watch
a man pull on the helmet of a bathing cap
and set out, swimming, for a farther shore?

Peter Kane Dufault

 A FIRST NIGHT

It's the first night, I suppose,
in more than eighty years
Hattie has slept alone. . . .
And outdoors, in the falling
snow, without bedclothes
or night light and none near
but the deaf sunken stone
were one to awake calling.

What could old Hattie have done
wrong, anyway? — Made raw-
milk cheese, rubbed eggs, admired
her rose-red Christmas cactus, and
rocked, looking out at one
more mid-February thaw,
drifts melting and dungwagon mired —
that now like a reprimand

she might have heard sixty-eight
or seventy years ago
(such as "Hattie thinks she is clever,
but will go to bed with boxed ears

and no supper"), she is told: "Tonight
you'll sleep with shoes on in the snow
in the cemetery and never
never wake up in a million years."

Douglas Dunn

 ELEGY FOR THE LOST PARISH

Dream, ploughman, of what agriculture brings,
Your eggs, your bacon to your greasy plate;
Then listen to the evening's thrush that sings
Exhilarated sadness and the intimate.

Your son's in Canada, growing his wheat
On fields the size of farms, and prosperous
On grain and granary. His world's replete
With life and love and house and happiness.

Dream, ploughman, of the lovely girl who died
So many summers gone, whose face will come
To you, call to you, and be deified
In sunlight on one cut chrysanthemum.

A nod of nettles flutters its green dust
Across small fields where you have mown the hay.
So wipe your brow, as on a scented gust
Your past flies in and will not go away.

Dream, ploughman, of old characters you've known
Who taught you things of scythe and horse and plough;
Of fields prepared, seed rhythmically sown,
Their ways of work that are forgotten now.

Remember, sir, and let them come to you
Out of your eye to mutter requiem,
Praising fidelities, the good of you.
Allow their consolations, cherish them

Into a privacy, as, with hand's slow shake
You reach towards your glass, your hands reach to
Where no one is or can be. Heartbreak,
Heartbreak and loneliness of virtue!

 WAR BLINDED

For more than sixty years he has been blind
Behind that wall, these trees, with terrible
Longevity wheeled in the sun and wind
On pathways of the soldiers' hospital.

For half that time his story's troubled me —
That showroom by the ferry, where I saw
His basketwork, a touch-turned filigree
His fingers coaxed from charitable straw;

Or how he felt when young, enlisting at
Recruiting tables on the football pitch,
To end up slumped across a parapet,
His eye-blood running in a molten ditch;

Or how the light looked when I saw two men,
One blind, one in a wheelchair, in that park,
Their dignity, which I have not forgotten,
Which helps me struggle with this lesser dark.

That war's too old for me to understand
How he might think, nursed now in wards of want,
Remembering that day when his right hand
Gripped on the shoulder of the man in front.

Charles Edward Eaton

 THE LYNX

We draw our lives after ourselves in streams —
The hurly-burly, the raw, rough, the long silken passage,
The lynx poised on the rock above, the bathing girl of our
    high dreams.

Those creamy, creamy shoulders and the brilliant, piercing
    eyes,
The suntanned skin, the tawny fur, the tension of
    the leap —
Who told you beauty and the beast could never share the
    selfsame paradise?

Do not think that these associations do not come and go —

The woman with her long, blood-red fingernails, lethal too,
The lynx, purring, pensive, turned albino, changed in the
    mind, soft as snow.

The woman, rising in the rift, streams and streams with gold:
We keep on making up her myth, holding, holding, setting
    stasis on the cat,
As if we would not run the risk, rupture that quietus, until
    the story, manifold, is told.

The lynx will keep his amber tone, her breasts are almond-
    white —
See how the mind goes back and forth with just two figures
    to control:
Think how the dam will slack and overflow when we lie
    down at night.

We stream and stream, push on, ahead, beyond —

I only tell you this because the lady with the blood-red nails
may one day dive
Where the spill has left the maw of all reflection yawning in
the pond.

Daniel Mark Epstein

From HOMAGE TO MALLARMÉ

Author's Note: These selections were inspired by the prose poems "Plainte d'automne" and "Frisson d'hiver" by Stéphane Mallarmé. Though my lyrics draw upon themes and images from the French, they are written in fairly strict meter, for which Mallarmé could not be held responsible. Yet the poems owe their life to Mallarmé, to whose spirit they are humbly dedicated. They are presented as homage rather than imitation or interpretation of Mallarmé's poems.

THE BARREL ORGAN

Since my Vivian left me
to fly to another star —
Orion was it, Altair,
or the pale emerald, Venus?
— I have loved being alone.

All day I sit alone, but
for the cat, and one poet
of the Latin decadence.
Since my woman has gone
I love the legends of autumn:

slow days of September,
autumn's prologue, the hour
the sun rests before it goes,

when rays copper the walls
and redden the windowpanes;

the slowly fading echoes
of the last hours of Rome,
those languid poems that come
before Barbarian cries
and stammering Christian prose.

I was deep in one of those
I love, whose patches of rouge
thrill me more than the rose
flesh of a budding girl, and
plunging an idle finger

into the cat's black fur
I heard outside my window
the melancholy singing
of a barrel organ. Under
the tree whose leaves in spring

seem dreary since Vivian
passed by for the last time,
I heard the sorrowful engine
that turns dreams to despair.
Then I heard it murmuring

some cheerful, vulgar reprise
that once made the back streets gay.
Yet the tune reached into my soul
and called the tears to my eyes
as no ballad has ever done.

I sipped at that song like wine
and would not go to the window
to send down my coin ringing

for fear I might see the organ
was not alone in its singing.

 OLD TIMES

Spiderwebs on the casement,
the wardrobe is ancient too,
fading curtains, peeling chairs,
nothing you own is new.

Didn't you wish, my sister,
with a glance at time vanishing,
my poems might set in meter
"the grace of some fading thing"?

New objects displease us
and scare us with their cries;
their need to be worn out
taxes our energies.

Come close that German almanac,
the days it proclaims are dead.
Lie down on the threadbare carpet,
calm child, pillow my head

on your knees in that faded gown
and I will talk on and on
of old clocks and cracked furniture
till the fields and streets are gone

under the cold of night.
Are your thoughts wandering?
On top of the casement
spiderwebs are shivering.

James Fenton

 GOD, A POEM

A nasty surprise in a sandwich,
A drawing-pin caught in your sock,
The limpest of shakes from a hand which
You'd thought would be firm as a rock,

A serious mistake in a nightie,
A grave disappointment all round
Is all that you'll get from th'Almighty,
Is all that you'll get underground.

Oh he *said:* "If you lay off the crumpet
I'll see you alright in the end.
Just hang on until the last trumpet.
Have faith in me, chum — I'm your friend."

But if you remind him, he'll tell you:
"I'm sorry, I must have been pissed —
Though your name rings a sort of a bell. You
Should have guessed that I do not exist.

"I didn't exist at Creation,
I didn't exist at the Flood,
And I won't be around for Salvation
To sort out the sheep from the cud —

"Or whatever the phrase is. The fact is
In soteriological terms
I'm a crude existential malpractice
And you are a diet of worms.

"You're a nasty surprise in a sandwich.
You're a drawing-pin caught in my sock.

You're the limpest of shakes from a hand which
I'd have thought would be firm as a rock,

"You're a serious mistake in a nightie,
You're a grave disappointment all round —
That's all that you are," says th'Almighty,
"And that's all that you'll be underground."

David Ferry

 REREADING OLD WRITING

Looking back, the language scribbles.
What's hidden, having been said?
Almost everything? Thrilling to think
There was a secret there somewhere,
A bird singing in the heart's forest.

Two people sitting by a river;
Sunlight, shadow, some pretty trees;
Death dappling in the flowing water;
Beautiful to think about,
Romance inscrutable as music.

Out of the ground, in New Jersey, my mother's
Voice, toneless, wailing — beseeching?
Crying out nothing? A winter vapor,
Out of the urn, rising in the yellow
Air, an ashy smear on the page.

The quiet room floats on the waters,
Buoyed up gently on the daylight;
The branch I can see stirs a little;
Nothing to think about; writing
Is a way of being happy.

What's going to be in this place?
A person entering a room?
Saying something? Signaling?
Writing a formula on a blackboard.
Something not to be understood.

 CYTHERA

There they go, down to the fatal ship.
They know how beautiful they are.
The ship will sail very soon. The sea
Will cover them over very soon unknowingly.

Wave goodbye from the shore, children.
I can see how your faces change in the sight
Of their going away. Wave to them.

Their sails are of silk, they're very pretty.
The sunset is all smiles, radiance,
The hues of a first or last innocence.
You look hungry, children, tired, angry.

Very beautiful is the manner of their going.
Music is playing about the mast; their lovely faces
Look lovelier still compared to the angry children.

John Fuller

 SONATA

The body leaning slightly back, the arms held firm and straight
As if she found those first deliberate chords a heavy weight

Impelling sound to herald, like the raising of a curtain,
A massive concentration on the things we find uncertain,
And with a noble carelessness of what she there might find,
She starts upon her journey to the centre of the mind.

At first the notes are confident of all they understand,
As if the sum of human purpose lies beneath each hand.
The cadences of concord cross the measured page in pairs
As calmly as a couple might descend the morning stairs
Or children playing in a garden weave the air with thirds
As though for simple happiness their calls were those of birds.

But then her eyes perceive ahead a shift in the notation.
An *allargando* of regret, bereavement's modulation,
Reveals the theme's distinction to be that of comprehending
How every ravishment contains the sourness of pretending
That in our perfect virtue it may chance to last for ever,
If destiny so smiles upon our singular endeavour.

Its falling minims lucidly declare the fight will fail
To win ourselves the closure of the lucky fairy-tale.
The sober music now decides the battle has been done.
Its message to the pianist is that nothing has been won.
Not even sheer persistence in the struggle for expression
Ever deprives the darkness of the fullness of possession.

Descending octaves falter as the left hand turns the page
Revealing flocks of quavers beating wings against their cage.
The fingers fumble wildly in their effort to release
The soul that mocks their movements from the prison of
        the piece.
She offers it the freedom that its dumbness cannot learn
Though she bargains for its ransom, trying all the keys in
        turn.

The music turns to panic only stubbornness denies,
As if the fingers' questions forced the vagueness of replies,

Until with all the righteousness of having come so far
It thunders to exhaustion at the final double bar.
Her hands remain a moment on the flat and silent keys
And then she slowly places them together on her knees.

Her head is motionless and bowed, hair faintly disarranged.
The silence holds suspended everything her hands have
        changed,
In muted echoes from the mind of what the air has lost.
Her feet have quietly drawn back from the pedals, ankles
        crossed,
As if conclusion could admonish how the sound behaves
When granted independence from the locked and blackened
        staves.

This moment is what you or I, had we been there to hear,
Would call the grave illusion of the will to persevere,
Since all except our love for her has vanished like a vapour
And nothing is at rest, or certain, save the printed paper,
For love demands a truth the music has denied in vain
And what it said contented us, and will content again.

ST. SOPHIA

Two figures there beneath the dome, walking with similar
        pace,
Turned as the other turned, forward and back, in that empty
        space.

Turning on the heel, looking about, casual but intense,
With everything that might belong to a stranger's cautious
        grace.

Eyes like hands went out to the marble and stone and precise
        gold
On the walls where the guarding images left a broken trace.

In the narthex, in the galleries, in the side-aisles,
Up and down, as drawn to each other as to that echoing
    place.

As though it were the whole world, and I saw the man was
    myself
And he walked there with the woman and the woman had
    your face.

Reginald Gibbons

 HOPPY

Ancientest of cats, truest
model of decrepitude,
you shamble and push your own
sloppy shape across the room,
nosing the floor in your slow
unhappy step-by-step, and
with dollops of baby food
splashed around your whiskers, on
chin, on snout, and in one scarred
ear, don't you think it's gotten
crappy, this life, now the years
have slipped by, old Counselor?
You mop the rug with your tail,
you slap a tired paw against
the door, and turn dim yellow
eyes, flecked with a weariness
of having seen so much, back
over your jutting shoulder
to the faces that study
the exquisite mishap or

the dopey luck that has left
it to you — of all the world's
mopes and most unlikely wise,
prophets and poets — to stop
the bored chatter of these frail
merely human types and top
all their tiny, much-boasted
perseverances with your
pained, apocalyptic glance.

Dana Gioia

 ### CALIFORNIA HILLS IN AUGUST

I can imagine someone who found
these fields unbearable, who climbed
the hillside in the heat, cursing the dust,
cracking the brittle weeds underfoot,
wishing a few more trees for shade.

An Easterner especially, who would scorn
the meagerness of summer, the dry
twisted shapes of black elm,
scrub oak, and chaparral, a landscape
August has already drained of green.

One who would hurry over the clinging
thistle, foxtail, golden poppy,
knowing everything was just a weed,
unable to conceive that these trees
and sparse brown bushes were alive.

And hate the bright stillness of the noon
without wind, without motion,

the only other living thing
a hawk, hungry for prey, suspended
in the blinding, sunlit blue.

And yet how gentle it seems to someone
raised in a landscape short of rain —
the skyline of a hill broken by no more
trees than one can count, the grass,
the empty sky, the wish for water.

 THE NEXT POEM

How much better it seems now
than when it is finally done —
the unforgettable first line,
the cunning way the stanzas run.

The rhymes (for, yes, it will have rhymes)
almost inaudible at first,
an appetite not yet acknowledged
like the inkling of a thirst.

While gradually the form appears
as each line is coaxed aloud —
the architecture of a room
seen from the middle of a crowd.

The music that of common speech
but slanted so that each detail
sounds unexpected as a sharp
inserted in a simple scale.

No jumble box of imagery
dumped glumly in the reader's lap
or elegantly packaged junk
the unsuspecting must unwrap,

But words that could direct a friend
precisely to an unknown place,
those few unshakeable details
no confusion can erase.

And the real subject left unspoken
but unmistakeable to those
who don't expect a jungle parrot
in the black and white of prose.

How much better it seems now
than when it is finally written.
How hungrily one waits to feel
the bright lure seized, the old hook bitten.

Melissa Green

From THE SQUANICOOK ECLOGUES

More than novelty crooked its finger — silent, austere,
Deeper than trees beating their wings or the purblind stare
Of a black snake circumscribing a sapling's wrist.
Father carefully penciled facts, describing rust,
Habitat, genus, disease, but his meticulous chart
Of change didn't teach me to name the woods' mysterious
       heart.
Father, I'm frightened. Why are things so beautiful and sad?
My voice had dusted moss, like snow, without a sound.
Stern and tall, he cupped his chin. As if in pain
He paused, then reached into his pocket for a pen.
Don't ever make things up. Write only what you see.
Name the woods and you'll have named the world, he said.
He tore some pages off and handed me his pad.

I heard the current crimp, mimetic, on the pond,
And larch or beech or birds murmuring over me. The task
Was how to write *birch* when I saw the crumbling, pale tusk
Of a fallen mastodon bridging the path, or *ash,* when the
air
Was frenzied with the head of a neighbor's rain-black mare.
Sycamore waved at me like drowned Ophelia's hair.

Marilyn Hacker

 IMAGINARY TRANSLATION

For James Keilty

These two meet for dinner once a week
in the old city. Middle-aged and grey
with some distinction — one wrote a verse play
that revolutionary students speak
intensely of; the other left archives
of an obscure study for politics,
talks urgency to Ministers and tricks
reason from hotheads — they lead public lives
of private circumspection, and they drink
together Thursdays. Twenty years ago
in a strange port, for two weeks and four days
they were lovers. Or enemies. They clink
snifters, wax quotable near "Time," then go
home their discrete and solitary ways.

Donald Hall

 O CHEESE

In the pantry the dear dense cheeses, Cheddars and harsh
Lancashires; Gorgonzola with its magnanimous manner;
the clipped speech of Roquefort; and a head of Stilton
that speaks in a sensuous riddling tongue like Druids.

O cheeses of gravity, cheeses of wistfulness, cheeses
that weep continually because they know they will die.
O cheeses of victory, cheeses wise in defeat, cheeses
fat as a cushion, lolling in bed until noon.

Liederkranz ebullient, jumping like a small dog, noisy;
Pont l'Evêque intellectual, and quite well informed;
   Emmentaler
decent and loyal, a little deaf in the right ear;
and Brie the revealing experience, instantaneous and
   profound.

O cheeses that dance in the moonlight, cheeses
that mingle with sausages, cheeses of Stonehenge.
O cheeses that are shy, that linger in the doorway,
eyes looking down, cheeses spectacular as fireworks.

Reblochon openly sexual; Caerphilly like pine trees, small
at the timberline; Port du Salut in love; Caprice des Dieux
eloquent, tactful, like a thousand-year-old hostess;
and Dolcelatte, always generous to a fault.

O village of cheeses, I make you this poem of cheeses,
O family of cheeses, living together in pantries,
O cheeses that keep to your own nature, like a lucky couple,
this solitude, this energy, these bodies slowly dying.

❦ GRANITE AND GRASS

I

On Ragged Mountain birches twist from rifts in granite.
Great ledges show gray through sugarbush. Brown bears
doze all winter under granite outcroppings or in cellarholes
the first settlers walled with fieldstone.
Granite markers recline in high abandoned graveyards.

Although split by frost or dynamite, granite is unaltered;
earthquakes tumble boulders across meadows; glaciers
carry pebbles with them as they grind south
and melt north, scooping lakes for the Penacook's trout.
Stone bulks, reflects sunlight, bears snow, and persists.

When highway-makers cut through a granite hill, scoring
deep trench-sides with vertical drillings, they leave behind
glittering sculptures, monuments to the granite state
of nature, emblems of permanence
that we worship in daily disease, and discover in stone.

2

But when we climb Ragged Mountain past cordwood
          stumpage,
over rocks of a dry creekbed, in company of young hemlock,
only granite remains unkind. Uprising in summer, in woods
and high pastures, our sister the fern breathes, trembles,
and alters, delicate fronds outspread and separate.

The fox pausing for scent cuts holes in hoarfrost.
Quail scream in the fisher's jaw; then the fisher dotes.
The coy-dog howls, raising puppies that breed more puppies
to rip the throats of rickety deer in March.
The moose's antlers extend, defending his wife for a season.

Mother-and-father grass lifts in the forsaken meadow,
grows tall under sun and rain, uncut, turns yellow,

sheds seeds, and under assault of snow relents; in May
green generates again. When the bear dies, bees construct
honey from nectar of cinquefoil growing through rib-bones.

3

Ragged Mountain was granite before Adam divided.
Grass lives because it dies. If weary of discord
we gaze heavenward through the same eye that looks at us,
vision makes light of contradiction:
Granite is grass in the holy meadow of the soul's repose.

Tony Harrison

 BOOK ENDS I

Baked the day she suddenly dropped dead
we chew it slowly that last apple pie.

Shocked into sleeplessness you're scared of bed
We never could talk much, and now don't try.

You're like book ends, the pair of you, she'd say,
Hog that grate, say nothing, sit, sleep, stare . . .

The "scholar" me, you, worn out on poor pay,
only our silence made us seem a pair.

Not as good for staring in, blue gas,
too regular each bud, each yellow spike.

A night you need my company to pass
and she not here to tell us we're alike!

Your life's all shattered into smithereens.

Back in our silences and sullen looks,
for all the Scotch we drink, what's still between 's
not the thirty or so years, but books, books, books.

 CONFESSIONAL POETRY

For Jeffrey Wainwright

When Milton *sees* his "late espoused saint"
are we sure the ghost's wife 1 or 2?
Does knowing it's himself beneath the paint
make the Rembrandts truer or less true?

But your father was a simple working man,
they'll say, *and didn't speak in those full rhymes.*
His words when *they came would scarcely scan.*

Mi dad's did scan, like yours do, many times!

That quarrel then in Book Ends II *between*
one you still go on addressing as "mi dad"
and you, your father comes across as mean
but weren't the taunts you flung back just as bad?

We *had* a bitter quarrel in our cups
and there *were* words between us, yes,
I'm guilty, and the way I make it up 's
in poetry, and that much I confess.

 THE QUEEN'S ENGLISH

Last meal together, Leeds, the Queen's Hotel,
that grandish pile of swank in City Square.
Too posh for me! he said (though he dressed well)
If you weren't wi' me now ah'd nivver dare!

41

I knew that he'd decided that he'd die
not by the way he lingered in the bar,
nor by that look he'd give with one good eye,
nor the firmer handshake and the gruff *ta-ra,*
but when we browsed the station bookstall sales
he picked up *Poems from the Yorkshire Dales* —

'ere tek this un wi' yer to New York
to remind yer 'ow us gaffers used to talk.
It's up your street in't it? ah'll buy yer that!

The broken lines go through me speeding South —

As t'Doctor stopped to oppen woodland yat . . .
and
    wi' skill they putten wuds reet i' his mouth.

Seamus Heaney

 A PEACOCK'S FEATHER

For Daisy Garnett

Six days ago the water fell
To christen you, to work its spell
And wipe your slate, we hope, for good.
But now your life is sleep and food
Which, with the touch of love, suffice
You, Daisy, Daisy, English niece.

Gloucestershire: its prospects lie
Wooded and misty to my eye
Whose landscape, as your mother's was,

Is other than this mellowness
Of topiary, lawn and brick,
Possessed, untrespassed, walled, nostalgic.

I come from scraggy farm and moss,
Old patchworks that the pitch and toss
Of history have left dishevelled.
But here, for your sake, I have levelled
My cart-track voice to garden tones,
Cobbled the bog with Cotswold stones.

Ravelling strands of families mesh
In love-knots of two minds, one flesh.
The future's not our own. We'll weave
An in-law maze, we'll nod and wave
With trust but little intimacy —
So this is a billet-doux to say

That in a warm July you lay
Christened and smiling in Bradley
While I, a guest in your green court,
At a west window sat and wrote
Self-consciously in gathering dark.
I might as well be in Coole Park.

So before I leave your ordered home,
Let us pray. May tilth and loam,
Darkened with Celts' and Saxons' blood,
Breastfeed your love of house and wood —
Where I drop this for you, as I pass,
Like the peacock's feather on the grass.

Anthony Hecht

 THE DEODAND

What are these women up to? They've gone and strung
Drapes over the windows, cutting out light
And the slightest hope of a breeze here in mid-August.
Can this be simply to avoid being seen
By some prying *femme-de-chambre* across the boulevard
Who has stepped out on a balcony to disburse
Her dustmop gleanings on the summer air?
And what of these rugs and pillows, all haphazard,
Here in what might be someone's living room
In the swank, high-toned sixteenth *arrondissement?*
What would their fathers, husbands, *fiancés,*
Those pillars of the old *haute-bourgeoisie,*
Think of the strange charade now in the making?
Swathed in exotic finery, in loose silks,
Gauzy organzas with metallic threads,
Intricate Arab vests, brass ornaments
At wrist and ankle, those small sexual fetters,
Tight little silver chains, and bangled gold
Suspended like a coarse barbarian treasure
From soft earlobes pierced through symbolically,
They are preparing some *tableau vivant.*
One girl, consulting the authority
Of a painting, perhaps by Ingres or Delacroix,
Is reporting over her shoulder on the use
Of kohl to lend its dark, savage allurements.
Another, playing the slave-artisan's role,
Almost completely naked, brush in hand,
Attends to these instructions as she prepares
To complete the seductive shadowing of the eyes
Of the blonde girl who appears the harem favorite,
And who is now admiring these effects

In a mirror held by a fourth, a well-clad servant.
The scene simmers with Paris and women in heat,
Darkened and airless, perhaps with a faint hum
Of trapped flies, and a strong odor of musk.
For whom do they play at this hot indolence
And languorous vassalage? They are alone
With fantasies of jasmine and brass lamps,
Melons and dates and bowls of rose-water,
A courtyard fountain's firework blaze of prisms,
Its basin sown with stars and *poissons d'or,*
And a rude stable smell of animal strength,
Of leather thongs, hinting of violations,
Swooning lubricities and lassitudes.
What is all this but crude imperial pride,
Feminized, scented and attenuated,
The exploitation of the primitive,
Homages of romantic self-deception,
Mimes of submission glamorized as lust?
Have they no intimation, no recall
Of the once queen who liked to play at milkmaid,
And the fierce butcher-reckoning that followed
Her innocent, unthinking masquerade?
Those who will not be taught by history
Have as their curse the office to repeat it,
And for this little spiritual debauch
(Reported here with warm, exacting care
By Pierre Renoir in 1872 —
Apparently unnoticed by the girls,
An invisible voyeur, like you and me)
Exactions shall be made, an expiation,
A forfeiture. Though it take ninety years,
All the retributive iron of Racine
Shall answer from the raging heat of the desert.

In the final months of the Algerian war
They captured a very young French Legionnaire.

They shaved his head, decked him in a blonde wig,
Carmined his lips grotesquely, fitted him out
With long, theatrical false eyelashes
And a bright, loose-fitting skirt of calico,
And cut off all the fingers of both hands.
He had to eat from a fork held by his captors.
Thus costumed, he was taken from town to town,
Encampment to encampment, on a leash,
And forced to beg for his food with a special verse
Sung to a popular show tune of those days:
"*Donnez moi à manger de vos mains*
Car c'est pour vous que je fais ma petite danse;
Car je suis Madeleine, la putain,
Et je m'en vais le lendemain matin,
Car je suis La Belle France."

THE GHOST IN THE MARTINI

Over the rim of the glass
Containing a good martini with a twist
I eye her bosom and consider a pass,
Certain we'd not be missed

In the general hubbub.
Her lips, which I forgot to say, are superb,
Never stop babbling once (Aye, there's the rub)
But who would want to curb

Such delicious, artful flattery?
It seems she adores my work, the distinguished grey
Of my hair. I muse on the salt and battery
Of the sexual clinch, and say

Something terse and gruff
About the marked disparity in our ages.

She looks like twenty-three, though eager enough.
    As for the famous wages

    Of sin, she can't have attained
Even to union scale, though you never can tell.
Her waist is slender and suggestively chained,
    And things are going well.

    The martini does its job,
God bless it, seeping down to the dark old id.
("Is there no cradle, Sir, you would not rob?"
    Says ego, but the lid

    Is off. The word is Strike
While the iron's hot.) And now, ingenuous and gay,
She is asking me about what I was like
    At twenty. (Twenty, eh?)

    You wouldn't have liked me then,
I answer, looking carefully into her eyes.
I was shy, withdrawn, awkward, one of those men
    That girls seemed to despise,

    Moody and self-obsessed,
Unhappy, defiant, with guilty dreams galore,
Full of ill-natured pride, an unconfessed
    Snob and a thorough bore.

    Her smile is meant to convey
How changed or modest I am, I can't tell which,
When I suddenly hear someone close to me say,
    "You lousy son-of-a-bitch!"

    A young man's voice, by the sound,
Coming, it seems, from the twist in the martini.

"You arrogant, elderly letch, you broken-down
Brother of Apeneck Sweeney!

Thought I was buried for good
Under six thick feet of mindless self-regard?
Dance on my grave, would you, you galliard stud,
Silenus in leotard?

Well, summon me you did,
And I come unwillingly, like Samuel's ghost.
'All things shall be revealed that have been hid.'
There's something for you to toast!

You only got where you are
By standing upon my ectoplasmic shoulders,
And wherever that is may not be so high or far
In the eyes of some beholders.

Take, for example, me.
I have sat alone in the dark, accomplishing little,
And worth no more to myself, in pride and fee,
Than a cup of luke-warm spittle.

But honest about it, withal . . ."
("Withal," forsooth!) "Please not to interrupt.
And the lovelies went by, 'the long and the short
and the tall,'
Hankered for, but untupped.

Bloody monastic it was.
A neurotic mixture of self-denial and fear;
The verse halting, the cataleptic pause,
No sensible pain, no tear,

But an interior drip
As from an ulcer, where, in the humid deep

Center of myself, I would scratch and grip
    The wet walls of the keep,

    Or lie on my back and smell
From the corners the sharp, ammoniac, urine stink.
    'No *light, but rather darkness visible.*'
    And plenty of time to think.

    In that thick, fetid air
I talked to myself in giddy recitative:
'*I have been studying how I may compare*
    This prison where I live

    Unto the world . . .' I learned
Little, and was awarded no degrees.
Yet all that sunken hideousness earned
    Your negligence and ease.

    Nor was it wholly sick,
Having procured you a certain modest fame;
A devotion, rather, a grim device to stick
    To something I could not name."

    Meanwhile, she babbles on
About men, or whatever, and the juniper juice
Shuts up at last, having sung, I trust, like a swan.
    Still given to self-abuse!

    Better get out of here;
If he opens his trap again it could get much worse.
I touch her elbow, and, leaning toward her ear,
    Tell her to find her purse.

Geoffrey Hill

 VENI CORONABERIS

A Garland for Helen Waddell

The crocus armies from the dead
rise up; the realm of love renews
the battle it was born to lose,
though for a time the snows have fled

and old stones blossom in the south
with sculpted vine and psaltery
and half-effaced adultery
the bird-dung dribbling from its mouth;

and abstinence crowns all our care
with martyr-laurels for this day.
Towers and steeples rise away
into the towering gulfs of air.

From THE MYSTERY OF THE CHARITY OF
CHARLES PÉGUY

Dear lords of life, stump-toothed, with ragged breath,
throng after throng cast out upon the earth,
flesh into dust, who slowly come to use
dreams of oblivion in lieu of paradise,

push on, push on! — through struggle, exhaustion,
indignities of all kinds, the impious Christian
oratory, "vos morituri," through berserk fear,
laughing, howling, "servitude et grandeur"

in other words, in nameless gobbets thrown
up by the blast, names issuing from mouths
of the dying, with their dying breaths.
But rest assured, bristly-brave gentlemen

of Normandie and Loire. Death does you proud,
every heroic commonplace, "Amor,"
"Fidelitas," polished like old armour,
stamped forever into the featureless mud.

Poilus and sous-officiers who plod
to your lives' end, name your own recompense,
expecting nothing but the grace of France,
drawn to her arms, her august plenitude.

The blaze of death goes out, the mind leaps
for its salvation, is at once extinct;
its last thoughts tetter the furrows, distinct
in dawn twilight, caught on the barbed loops.

Whatever strikes and maims us it is not
fate, to our knowledge. En avant, Péguy!
The irony of advancement. Say "we
possess nothing; try to hold on to that."

From HYMNS TO OUR LADY OF CHARTRES

Eia, with handbells, jews' harps, risible
tuckets of salutation! Otherwise
gnashing and gnawing sound out your praise.
Salve regina! Visible, invisible,

powers, presences, in and beyond the blue
glass, radiantly-occluded Sion, pour
festal light at the feet of the new poor,
scavengers upon grace, and of your true

servant Péguy who cries out from the crowd
where your bienpensants clatter to adore
la Dame du Pilier and her wooden stare.
The priests go nodding by, dainty and shrewd,

and virgins with trim lamps devoutly oiled,
to do the honours of your mysteries.
Through what straits might we come to worship this,
and kneel before you, and be reconciled,

among the flowering lances, the heathen
gold phalanxes of flame; at the high seats
where Mercy is redeemed from its own threats;
with dumb-struck martyrs trumpeted to heaven?

Edward Hirsch

 FAST BREAK

In memory of Dennis Turner, 1946–1984

A hook shot kisses the rim and
hangs there, helplessly, but doesn't drop,

and for once our gangly starting center
boxes out his man and times his jump

perfectly, gathering the orange leather
from the air like a cherished possession

and spinning around to throw a strike
to the outlet who is already shoveling

an underhand pass toward the other guard
scissoring past a flat-footed defender

who looks stunned and nailed to the floor
in the wrong direction, trying to catch sight

of a high, gliding dribble and a man
letting the play develop in front of him

in slow motion, almost exactly
like a coach's drawing on the blackboard,

both forwards racing down the court
the way that forwards should, fanning out

and filling the lanes in tandem, moving
together as brothers passing the ball

between them without a dribble, without
a single bounce hitting the hardwood

until the guard finally lunges out
and commits to the wrong man

while the power-forward explodes past them
in a fury, taking the ball into the air

by himself now and laying it gently
against the glass for a lay-up,

but losing his balance in the process,
inexplicably falling, hitting the floor

with a wild, headlong motion
for the game he loved like a country

and swiveling back to see an orange blur
floating perfectly through the net.

John Hollander

 THE OLD GUITAR

I take down the old guitar from the wall,
Instrument of the idle, and silent —
What can it say for me? I only hear
An ailing wind blow through my dead fingers.

I feel only the chill of silence there.
And just as well — suppose I plucked the fruit
Of trellised chords: how would this hollow shell
Shaped like an absent body, then resound?

Wildly, like the roaring wind's melody,
Only an echo of its malady.
Like the blackened waters of a midnight
River running deep inside a closed book.

Richard Howard

From ITHACA: THE PALACE AT FOUR A.M.

 LAST WORDS

What I "have to do" has nothing to do
with what I have — or with doing, either.

You tell me I have you. Evidently
you can't imagine what it means to live
inside a legend — scratch a Hero and
you're likely to find almost anything!

Having scratched, I found you. Was I surprised?
Once her womb becomes a cave of the winds
which appears to be uninhabited,
there are no surprises for a woman —
she has survived them all. But at the loom
I learned that even you were ignorant,

crafty Ulysses! Weaving taught me: our
makeshifts become our mode until there is
no such thing as *meanwhile*. Not craft but art!
So you see, I must ravel the design
all over again: there is no end in sight.
Ulysses home? You don't come home at all,

wandering will do that, though I say it
who never left. The loom's my odyssey —
dare I call it my penelopiad?
You think you were asleep just now, don't you,
after those homecoming exertions? But
you were never here at all, my husband:

the sea still has you — I heard you insist
you were No-one. No one? How many times
you sighed "Circe" in that light sleep of yours:
she must have had her points, old what's-her-name.
You snored but sirens sang, and when the moon
silvered our bed you seemed to feel the sun

depositing tiny crystals of salt
all over your old skin. You were away.
That was your weaving — and my wandering.
The suitors are dead, your bow is a prop,

but neither of *us* is present. Let me
give you some peace at this ungodly hour . . .

Be patient — having found or feigned this much,
perhaps the two of us can fool the world
into seeing that famous genre scene:
The King and Queen Restored. It's abstinence
that makes the heart meander: you're at sea,
I worry this web. Lover, welcome home!

Andrew Hudgins

 THE PERSISTENCE OF NATURE IN OUR LIVES

You find them in the darker woods
occasionally — those swollen lumps
of fungus, twisted, moist, and yellow —
but when they show up on the lawn
it's like they've tracked me home. In spring
the persistence of nature in our lives
rises from below, drifts from above.
The pollen settles on my skin
and waits for me to bloom, trying
to work green magic on my flesh.
They're indiscriminate, these firs.
They'll mate with anything. A great
green-yellow cloud of pollen sifts
across the house. The waste of it
leaves nothing out — not even men.
The pollen doesn't care I'm not
a tree. The golden storm descends.
Wind lifts it from the branches, lofts
it in descending arches of need

and search, a grainy yellow haze
that settles over everything
as if it's all the same. I love
the utter waste of pollen, a scum
of it on every pond and puddle.
It rides the ripples and, when they dry,
remains, a line of yellow dust
zigzagging in the shape of waves.
One night, perhaps a little drunk,
I stretched out on the porch, watching
the Milky Way. At dawn I woke
to find a man-shape on the hard
wood floor, outlined in pollen — a sharp
spread-eagle figure drawn there like
the body at a murder scene.
Except for that spot, the whole damn house
glittered, green-gold. I wandered out
across the lawn, my bare feet damp
with dew, the wet ground soft, forgiving,
beneath my step. I understood
I am, as much as anyone,
the golden beast who staggers home,
in June, beneath the yearning trees.

Donald Justice

 CHILDREN WALKING HOME FROM SCHOOL
THROUGH GOOD NEIGHBORHOOD

They are like figures held in some glass ball,
One of those in which, when shaken, snowstorms occur;
But this one is not yet shaken.
     And they go unaccompanied still,

Out along this walkway between two worlds,
This almost swaying bridge.
     October sunlight checkers their path;
It frets their cheeks and bare arms now with shadow
Almost too pure to signify itself.
And they progress slowly, somewhat lingeringly,
Independent, yet moving all together,
Like polyphonic voices that crisscross
In short-lived harmonies.

     Today, a few stragglers.
One, a girl, stands there with hands spaced out, so —
A gesture in a story. Someone's school notebook spills,
And they bend down to gather up the loose pages.
(Bright sweaters knotted at the waist; solemn expressions.)
Not that they would shrink or hold back from what may
     come,
For now they all at once run to meet it, a little swirl of
     colors,
Like the leaves already blazing and falling farther north.

PSALM AND LAMENT

In memory of my mother (1897–1974)
Hialeah, Florida

The clocks are sorry, the clocks are very sad.
One stops, one goes on striking the wrong hours.

And the grass burns terribly in the sun,
The grass turns yellow secretly at the roots.

Now suddenly the yard chairs look empty, the sky looks
     empty,
The sky looks vast and empty.

Out on Red Road the traffic continues; everything continues.
Nor does memory sleep; it goes on.

Out spring the butterflies of recollection,
And I think that for the first time I understand

The beautiful ordinary light of this patio
And even perhaps the dark rich earth of a heart.

(The bedclothes, they say, had been pulled down.
I will not describe it. I do not want to describe it.

No, but the sheets were drenched and twisted.
They were the very handkerchiefs of grief.)

Let summer come now with its schoolboy trumpets and
            fountains.
But the years are gone, the years are finally over.

And there is only
This long desolation of flower-bordered sidewalks

That runs to the corner, turns, and goes on,
That disappears and goes on

Into the black oblivion of a neighborhood and a world
Without billboards or yesterdays.

Sometimes a sad moon comes and waters the roof tiles.
But the years are gone. There are no more years.

IN MEMORY OF THE UNKNOWN POET,
ROBERT BOARDMAN VAUGHN

> But the essential advantage for a poet is not, to have a beautiful
> world with which to deal: it is to be able to see beneath
> both beauty and ugliness; to see the boredom, and the horror,
> and the glory.
> — *T. S. Eliot*

It was his story. It would always be his story.
It followed him; it overtook him finally —
The boredom, and the horror, and the glory.

Probably at the end he was not yet sorry,
Even as the boots were brutalizing him in the alley.
It was his story. It would always be his story,

Blown on a blue horn, full of sound and fury,
But signifying, O signifying magnificently
The boredom, and the horror, and the glory.

I picture the snow as falling without hurry
To cover the cobbles and the toppled ashcans completely.
It was his story. It would always be his story.

Lately he had wandered between St. Mark's Place and the
        Bowery,
Already half a spirit, mumbling and muttering sadly.
O the boredom, and the horror, and the glory!

All done now. But I remember the fiery
Hypnotic eye and the raised voice blazing with poetry.
It was his story and would always be his story —
The boredom, and the horror, and the glory.

X. J. Kennedy

 HANGOVER MASS

Of all sins of the flesh, that reprobate
    My father had but one, and it had class:
To sip tea of a Sunday till so late
    We'd barely make it up to Drunkards' Mass.

After a sermon on the wiles of booze,
    The bread and wine transformed with decent haste,
Quickly the priest would drive us forth to graze
    Where among churchyard flocks I'd get a taste

Of chronic loneliness. Red-rimmed of eye,
    Quaking of hand, old men my old man knew
Would congregate to help bad time go by:
    Stout Denny Casey, gaunt Dan Donahue

Who'd mention girls with withering contempt,
    Each man long gone past hope to meet his match
Unless in what he drank all night, or dreamt.
    Each knee I stared at cried out for a patch.

A sealed half-pint, I'd stand there keeping mum
    Till, bored to death, I'd throw a fit of shakes.
Then with relief we'd both go stepping home
    Over sidewalk cracks' imaginary snakes.

 TERSE ELEGY FOR J. V. CUNNINGHAM

Now Cunningham, who rhymed by fits and starts,
So loath to gush, most sensitive of hearts —
Else why so hard-forged a protective crust? —

Is brought down to the unresponding dust.
Though with a slash a Pomp's gut he could slit,
On his own flesh he worked his weaponed wit
And penned with patient skill and lore immense,
Prodigious mind, keen ear, rare common sense,
Only those words he could crush down no more
Like matter pressured to a dwarf star's core.
May one day eyes unborn wake to esteem
His steady, baleful, solitary gleam.
Poets may come whose work more quickly strikes
Love, and yet — ah, who'll live to see his likes?

Richard Kenney

 LA BREA

Early

It is very early now, no light yet, nor
sensation, apart from simple motions of waking:
discomfort in the chill air, the stiff walk
quick across cold floorboards, razor,
brushed lather and warm tap water off
my cheeks — the feel of bare wool on wrists
and throat — the hiss of the stove, and white coffee.
Alone in this house, I wonder if *tabula rasa*
ever existed at all. Lake Champlain looks flat,
black by starlight; even the sheaved winds
are flat as feathers on a sleeping raven's wing —
Later, forecast rains will toss down Smuggler's Notch
in silver skirtveils, hiss across the flatiron
lake like drops on a woodstove, into the night —

Tranquility

and hideous broom-flaps here, unfolding condors
knuckled to the vague bed rail, and hung door-
jamb anthropoid with clothes — In this appalling
light even physical objects fail, conform to older
recollection, night's La Brea, the glossy oil-pools. . . .
By breakfast all grotesques have quit their roaring,
pawing at the sky for light and release, followed
their immense tracks down sinkholes of their own
muddling until the only evidence
of dreams is gone, erratic haloes ravens
figured, just askim the water, rings, rings,
and love, your slender unstockinged feet scarcely
and always rough the nap of a newswept carpet
still, and this is not tranquility, not yet —

Stanley Kunitz

 THE WELLFLEET WHALE

*A few summers ago, on Cape Cod, a whale foundered on
the beach, a sixty-three-foot finback whale. When the tide
went out, I approached him. He was lying there, in monstrous
desolation, making the most terrifying noises — rumbling —
groaning. I put my hands on his flanks and I could feel the
life inside him. And while I was standing there, suddenly he
opened his eye. It was a big, red, cold eye, and it was staring
directly at me. A shudder of recognition passed between us.
Then the eye closed forever. I've been thinking about whales
ever since.*
        — Journal entry

1

You have your language too,
    an eerie medley of clicks
    and hoots and trills,
location-notes and love calls,
    whistles and grunts. Occasionally,
    it's like furniture being smashed,
or the creaking of a mossy door,
    sounds that all melt into a liquid
    song with endless variations,
as if to compensate
    for the vast loneliness of the sea.
    Sometimes a disembodied voice
breaks in, as if from distant reefs,
    and it's as much as one can bear
    to listen to its long mournful cry,
a sorrow without name, both more
    and less than human. It drags
    across the ear like a record
running down.

2

No wind. No waves. No clouds.
    Only the whisper of the tide,
    as it withdrew, stroking the shore,
a lazy drift of gulls overhead,
    and tiny points of light
    bubbling in the channel.
It was the tag-end of summer.
    From the harbor's mouth
    you coasted into sight,
flashing news of your advent,
    the crescent of your dorsal fin
    clipping the diamonded surface.
We cheered at the sign of your greatness
    when the black barrel of your head
    erupted, ramming the water,

and you flowered for us
  in the jet of your spouting.

3
All afternoon you swam
  tirelessly round the bay,
    with such an easy motion,
the slightest downbeat of your tail,
  an almost imperceptible
    undulation of your flippers,
you seemed like something poured,
  not driven; you seemed
    to marry grace with power.
And when you bounded into air,
  slapping your flukes,
    we thrilled to look upon
pure energy incarnate
  as nobility of form.
    You seemed to ask of us
not sympathy, or love,
  or understanding,
    but awe and wonder.

That night we watched you
  swimming in the moon.
    Your back was molten silver.
We guessed your silent passage
  by the phosphorescence in your wake.
    At dawn we found you stranded on the rocks.

4
There came a boy and a man
  and yet other men running, and two
    schoolgirls in yellow halters
and a housewife bedecked
  with curlers, and whole families in beach
    buggies with assorted yelping dogs.

The tide was almost out.
    We could walk around you,
        as you heaved deeper into the shoal,
crushed by your own weight,
    collapsing into yourself,
        your flippers and your flukes
quivering, your blowhole
    spasmodically bubbling, roaring.
        In the pit of your gaping mouth
you bared your fringework of baleen,
    a thicket of horned bristles.
        When the Curator of Mammals
arrived from Boston
    to take samples of your blood
        you were already oozing from below.
Somebody had carved his initials
    in your flank. Hunters of souvenirs
        had peeled off strips of your skin,
a membrane thin as paper.
    You were blistered and cracked by the sun.
        The gulls had been pecking at you.
The sound you made was a hoarse and fitful bleating.

What drew us, like a magnet, to your dying?
    You made a bond between us,
        the keepers of the nightfall watch,
who gathered in a ring around you,
    boozing in the bonfire light.
        Toward dawn we shared with you
your hour of desolation,
    the huge lingering passion
        of your unearthly outcry,
as you swung your blind head
    toward us and laboriously opened
        a bloodshot, glistening eye,
in which we swam with terror and recognition.

5

Voyager, chief of the pelagic world,
    you brought with you the myth
        of another country, dimly remembered,
where flying reptiles
        lumbered over the steaming marshes
            and trumpeting thunder lizards
wallowed in the reeds.
    While empires rose and fell on land,
        your nation breasted the open main,
rocked in the consoling rhythm
        of the tides. Which ancestor first plunged
            head-down through zones of colored twilight
to scour the bottom of the dark?
    You ranged the North Atlantic track
        from Port-of-Spain to Baffin Bay,
edging between the ice-floes
        through the fat of summer,
            lob-tailing, breaching, sounding,
grazing in the pastures of the sea
        on krill-rich orange plankton
            crackling with life.
You prowled down the continental shelf,
    guided by the sun and stars
        and the taste of alluvial silt
on your way southward
        to the warm lagoons,
            the tropic of desire,
where the lovers lie belly to belly
        in the rub and nuzzle of their sporting;
            and you turned, like a god in exile,
out of your wide primeval element,
        delivered to the mercy of time.
    Master of the whale-roads,
let the white wings of the gulls
        spread out their cover.

You have become like us,
disgraced and mortal.

Brad Leithauser

 ANGEL

There between the riverbank
and half-submerged tree trunk
it's a kind of alleyway
inviting loiterers —
    in this case, water striders.

Their legs, twice body-length, dent
the surface, but why they don't
sink is a transparent riddle:
the springs of their trampoline
    are nowhere to be seen.

Inches and yet far below, thin
as compass needles, almost, min-
nows flicker through the sun's
tattered netting, circling past
    each other as if lost.

Enter an angel, in
the form of a dragon-
fly, an apparition whose
coloring, were it not real,
    would scarcely be possible:

see him, like a sparkler,
tossing lights upon the water,

surplus greens, reds, milky
blues, and violets blended
    with ebony. Suspended

like a conductor's baton,
he hovers, then goes the one
way no minnow points: straight
up, into that vast solution
    of which he's a concentrate.

 THE TIGERS OF NANZEN-JI

These light-footed, celebrated
        cats, created
on gold-leaf screens by a man
    who'd never seen a tiger
        (there were none in Japan),
who worked, as he'd been taught,
from pelts, and from paintings brought
    from distant, brilliant China,

wander an extraordinary
        maze whose very
air's alive, alit with breeze-
    borne inebriants. It's a place
    of tumbled boundaries
and whetted penchants, in which
big-chested brutes whose eyes are rich
    outsize eggs of burnished gold,

whose coats are cloudy, glowing
        masses flowing
behind an emerald palisade
    of bamboo and the row
        of darker palings made

by their own sable bands, glide
fatefully in the failing light, wide
    mouths agape and bared teeth flashing.

    It's an hour of satisfying
        runs and flying
ambitions, as gravity's
    traction relaxes a little
        and hunting tigers freeze
into a fine, deepening
tensity, muscles marshaling
    toward that signal opportune instant

    when the commanding soul emerges:
        Now —
            Now, it urges,
and the breaking body slides
    upon the air's broad back
        and hangs there, rides and rides
with limbs outstretched — but claws
bedded in their velvet-napped paws,
    for there will be no killings tonight.

    All bloodshed is forbidden
        here. . . .
            That's the hidden
message of these grounds, which threads
    like a stream around the pines
        and rocks and iris-beds.
The danger's all a bluff, an
artful dumb show staged by a clan-
destine family of tigers

    with Chinese dragon faces,
        whose grimaces
and slashing, cross-eyed glances serve
    to conceal the grins that beckon

you into the preserve
of a rare, ferociously
playful mind. Enter. You are free
from harm here. There's nothing to fear.

William Logan

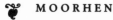 MOORHEN

To have
red mouth and green shanks
like a sidewalk hooker
come up through the ranks
of weeds does not disqualify
you from honorary membership
in the upper class,
the community of spies,
or any lowly clan
not put off by outer feathers that
conceal the inward man.

Or hen in this case, unsexed
like Lady Macbeth or the Chairs;
though no more rude than the next
species downstream
you've never grown fat
like a capon on chocolate éclairs.
The dictionary calls you
a *common* gallinule,
an insult, I suppose.
Your family has elongated
webless toes,

but all families have problems,
marital or genetic,

in search of a mastering art
or a convenient aesthetic.
　　Admiral, it's an admirable life
asleep on the water
　　above crepuscular plants
and miniature pike
　　that never need to be tended
and never go out on strike.
　　You nose among the rank

　　roots, washed white and ghostly,
grasses weave on the bank,
　　where bugs, I assume, have costly
apartments, and are always behind with the rent.
　　And you, you're the rent collector,
dealing in first-born sons
　　and daughters, grannies, long-lost cousins,
virtually everyone.
　　How convenient to be a ridiculous
rapacious insectivore,
　　much better than being dependent

　　on a grocery store.
How convenient to maintain a demeanor:
　　when chased or thwarted by fear
you sail between the weeds
　　and disappear.
Did you descend from the moors,
　　purple and lush with heather,
far away from the stores
　　and with indifferent weather?
Better here in the lowlands
　　full of *noblesse oblige;*

　　where the rats own baby grands
Inland Revenue never lays siege.

Reduced to one expression,
call it amused but grave,
    that achieves its own lesson
on the etiquette of where to behave,
    you plod with unwieldy grace
as if the ditch were a minefield
    and not a froth of lace.
I feel estranged
    that way too, sometimes — we all do, hen,

    but what's the use?
You'll wake tomorrow and the ditch
    will not have changed.

Derek Mahon

 TABLE TALK

You think I am your servant but you are wrong —
The service lies with you. During your long
Labours at me, I am the indulgent wood,
Tolerant of your painstaking ineptitude.
Your poems were torn from me by violence;
I am here to receive your homage in dark silence.

Remembering the chain-saw surgery and the seaward groan,
Like a bound and goaded exodus from Babylon,
I pray for a wood-spirit to make me dance,
To scare you shitless and upset your balance,
Destroy the sedate poise with which you pour
Forth your ephemeral stream of literature.

When I was a pine and lived in a cold climate
I listened to leaf-rumours about our fate;
But I have come a long way since then
To watch the sun glint on your reflective pen.
The hurt I do resent, and my consolation
Will be the unspoilt paper when you have gone.

And yet I love you, even in your ignorance,
Perhaps because at last you are making sense —
Talking to me, not through me, recognizing
That it is I alone who let you sing
Wood music. Hitherto shadowy and dumb,
I speak to you now as your indispensable medium.

A GARAGE IN CO. CORK

Surely you paused at this roadside oasis
In your nomadic youth, and saw the mound
Of never-used cement, the curious faces,
The soft-drink ads and the uneven ground
Rainbowed with oily puddles, where a snail
Had scrawled its slimy, phosphorescent trail.

Like a frontier store-front in an old western
It might have nothing behind it but thin air,
Building materials, fruit boxes, scrap iron,
Dust-laden shrubs and coils of rusty wire,
A cabbage-white fluttering in the sodden
Silence of an untended kitchen garden.

Nirvana! But the cracked panes reveal a dark
Interior echoing with the cries of children.
Here in this quiet corner of Co. Cork
A family ate, slept, and watched the rain
Dance clean and cobalt the exhausted grit
So that the mind shrank from the glare of it.

Where did they go? South Boston? Cricklewood?
Somebody somewhere thinks of this as home,
Remembering the old pumps where they stood,
Antique now, squirting juice into a chrome
Lagonda or a dung-caked tractor while
A cloud swam on a cloud-reflecting tile.

Surely a whitewashed sun-trap at the back
Gave way to hens, wild thyme, and the first few
Shadowy yards of an overgrown cart-track,
Tyres in the branches such as Noah knew —
Beyond, a swoop of mountain where you heard,
Disconsolate in the haze, a single blackbird.

Left to itself, the functional will cast
A death-bed glow of picturesque abandon.
The intact antiquities of the recent past,
Dropped from the retail catalogues, return
To the materials that gave rise to them
And shine with a late sacramental gleam.

A god who spent the night here once rewarded
Natural courtesy with eternal life —
Changing to petrol pumps, that they be spared
For ever there, an old man and his wife.
The virgin who escaped his dark design
Sanctions the townland from her prickly shrine.

We might be anywhere — in the Dordogne,
Iquitos, Bethlehem — wherever the force
Of gravity secures houses and the sun
Selects this fan-blade of the universe
Decelerating while the fates devise
What outcome for the dawdling galaxies?

But we are in one place and one place only,
One of the milestones of earth-residence

Unique in each particular, the thinly
Peopled hinterland serenely tense —
Not in the hope of a resplendent future
But with a sure sense of its intrinsic nature.

J. D. McClatchy

 AT A READING

Anthony Hecht's

And what if now I told you this, let's say,
By telephone. Would you imagine me
Talking to myself in an empty room,
Watching myself in the window talking,
My lips moving silently, birdlike,
On the glass, or because superimposed
On it, among the branches of the tree
Inside my head? As if what I had to say
To you were in these miniatures of the day,
When it is last night's shadow shadows
Have made bright.
                        Between us at the reading —
You up by that child's coffin of a podium,
The new poem, your "Transparent Man," to try,
And my seat halfway back in the dimmed house —
That couple conspicuous in the front row
You must have thought the worst audience:
He talked all the while you read, she hung
On *his* every word, not one of yours.
The others, rapt fan or narcolept,
Paid their own kind of attention, but not
Those two, calm in disregard, themselves

A commentary running from the point.
Into putdown? you must have wondered,
Your poem turned into an example, the example
Held up, if not to scorn, to a glaring
Spot of misunderstanding, some parody
Of the original idea, its clear-obscure
Of passageways and the mirrory reaches
Of beatitude where the dead select
Their patience and love discloses itself
Once and for all.
          But you kept going.
I saw you never once look down at them,
As if by speaking *through* her you might
Save the girl for yourself and lead her back
To *your* poem, *your* words to lose herself in,
Who sat there as if at a bedside, watching,
In her shift of loud, clenched roses, her hands
Balled under her chin, a heart in her throat
And gone out in her gaze to the friend
Beside her. How clearly she stood out
Against everything going on in front of us.

It was then I realized that she was deaf
And the bearded boy, a line behind you,
Translating the poem for her into silence,
Helping it out of its disguise of words,
A story spilled expressionless from the lip
Of his mimed exaggerations, like last words
Unuttered but mouthed in the mind and formed
By what, through the closed eyelid's archway,
Has been newly seen, those words she saw
And seeing heard — or not heard but let sink in,
Into a darkness past anyone's telling,
There between us.
          What she next said,
The bald childless woman in your fable,

She said, head turned, out the window
Of her hospital room to trees across the way,
The leaflorn beech and the sycamores
That stood like enlargements of the vascular
System of the brain, minds meditating on
The hill, the weather, the storm of leukemia
In the woman's bloodstream, the whole lot
Of it "a riddle beyond the eye's solution,"
These systems, anarchies, ends not our own.

The girl had turned her back to you by then,
Her eyes intent on the thickness of particulars,
The wintery emphasis of that woman's dying,
Like facing a glass-bright, amplified stage,
Too painful not to follow back to a source
In the self. And like the girl, I found myself
Looking at the boy, your voice suddenly
Thrown into him, as he echoed the woman's
Final rendering, a voice that drove upward
Onto the lampblack twigs just beyond her view
To look back on her body there, on its page
Of monologue. The words, as they came —
Came from you, from the woman, from the voice
In the trees — were his then, the poem come
From someone else's lips, as it can.

James Merrill

 LOSING THE MARBLES

I

Morning spent looking for my calendar —
Ten whole months mislaid, name and address,

A groaning board swept clean . . .
And what were we talking about at lunch? Another
Marble gone. These latter years, Charmides,
Will see the mind eroded featureless.

Ah. We'd been imagining our "heaven"'s.
Mine was to be an acrobat in Athens
Back when the Parthenon —
Its looted nymphs and warriors pristine
By early light or noon light — dwelt
Upon the city like a philosopher,
Who now — well, you have seen.

Here in the gathering dusk one could no doubt
"Rage against the dying of the light."
But really — rage? (So like the Athens press,
Breathing fire to get the marbles back.)
These dreamy blinkings out
Strike me as grace, if I may say so,
Capital punishment,
Yes, but of utmost clemency at work,
Whereby the human stuff, ready or not,
Tumbles, one last drumroll, into thyme,
Out of time, with just the fossil quirk
At heart to prove — hold on, don't tell me . . . What?

II

Driving its silver car into the room,
The storm mapped a new country's dry and wet —
Oblivion's ink-blue rivulet.
Mascara running, worksheet to worksheet
Clings underfoot, exchanging the wrong words.
The right ones, we can only trust, will somehow
Return to the tongue's tip,
Weary particular and straying theme,
Invigorated by their dip.

Invigorated! Gasping, shivering
Under our rough towels, never did they dream — !
Whom mouth-to-mouth resuscitation by
Even your Golden Treasury won't save,
They feel their claim
On *us* expiring, starved to macron, breve,
Those fleshless ribs, a beggar's frame. . . .
From the brainstorm to this was one far cry.

Long work of knowing and hard play of wit
Take their toll like any virus.
Old-timers, cured, wade ankle-deep in sky.

Meanwhile, come evening, to sit
Feverishly restoring the papyrus.

III

body, favorite
      gleaned,   at the
              vital
     frenzy—

act and moonshaft, peaks
                stiffening
     Unutter[able]
   the beloved's

                    slowly
    sustained in the deep   fixed
        summer nights
   or,

     scornful   Ch[arm]ides,
       decrepitude

Now, however, that
figures also

                        body everywhere
                    plunders and
    what we cannot — from the hut's lintel
                flawed

                                white as
    sliced turnip   the field's brow.
            our old poets
        wanderings

    home   palace, temple
        having   of those blue foothills
            no further   clear
                    fancy[.]

IV

Seven ages make a crazy quilt
Out of the famous web. Yet should milk spilt
(As when in Rhetoric one's paragraph
Was passed around and each time cut by half,
From eighty words to forty, twenty, ten,
Before imploding in a puff of Zen)
White out the sense and mutilate the phrase,
My text is Mind no less than Mallarmé's.
My illustration? The Cézanne oil sketch
Whose tracts of raw, uncharted canvas fetch
As much per square inch as the fruit our cloyed
Taste prizes for its bearing on the void.
Besides, Art furnishes a counterfeit
Heaven wherein ideas escape the fate
Their loyal adherents — brainwashed, so to speak,
By acid rain (more diatribes in Greek) —
Conspicuously don't. We diehard few

Embark for London on the QE 2.
Here mornings can be spent considering ours
Of long ago, removed and mute, like stars
(*Un*like vociferous Melina, once
A star herself, now Minister of Stunts).
Removed a further stage, viewed from this high wire
Between the elegiac and the haywire,
They even so raise questions. Does the will-
To-structural-elaboration still
Flute up from shifting dregs of would-be rock
Glints of a future colonnade and frieze?
Do higher brows unknit within the block,
And eyes whose Phidias and Pericles
Are eons hence make out through crystal skeins
Wind-loosened tresses and the twitch of reins?
Ah, not for long will marble school the blood
Against the warbling sirens of the flood.
All stone once dressed asks to be worn. The foam-
Pale seaside temple, like a palindrome,
Had quietly laid its plans for stealing back.
What are the Seven Wonders now? A pile
Of wave-washed pebbles. Topless women smile,
Picking the smoothest, rose-flawed white or black,
Which taste of sunlight on moon-rusted swords,
To use as men upon their checkerboards.

  v
The body, favorite trope of our youthful poets . . .
  With it they gleaned, as at the sibyl's tripod,
   insight too prompt and vital for words.
    Her sleepless frenzy —

cataract and moonshaft, peaks of sheer fire at dawn,
  dung-dusted violets, the stiffening dew —
   said it best. Unutterable, too,
    was the beloved's,

save through the index of refraction a fair, slowly
turned head sustained in the deep look that fixed him.
From then on, veining summer nights with
flickering ichor,

he had joined an élite scornful — as were, Charmides,
your first, chiselled verses — of decrepitude
in any form. Now, however, that
their figures also

begin to slip the mind — while the body everywhere
with peasant shrewdness plunders and puts to use
what we cannot — from the hut's lintel
gleams one flawed image;

another, cast up by frost or earthquake, shines white as
sliced turnip from a furrow on the field's brow.
Humbly our old poets knew to make
wanderings into

homecomings of a sort — harbor, palace, temple, all
having been quarried out of those blue foothills
no further off, these last clear autumn
days, than infancy.

VI

Who gazed into the wrack till
Inspiration glowed,
Deducing from one dactyl
The handmaiden, the ode?

Or when aphasia skewered
The world upon a word,
Who was the friend, the steward,
Who bent his head, inferred,

Then filled the sorry spaces
With pattern and intent,
A syntax of lit spaces
From the impediment?

                     No matter, these belated
Few at least are back. And, thanks
To their little adventure, never so
Brimming with jokes and schemes,
Fussed over, fêted
By all but their fellow-saltimbanques —
Though, truth to tell,
Who by now doesn't flip
Hourly from someone's upper story
("That writer . . . no, on shipboard . . . wait . . .
        Charmides?")
And come to, clinging to the net?
And yet, and yet,
Here in the afterglow
It almost seems
Death has forgotten us
— As the old lady said to Fontenelle.
                      And he,
A cautionary finger to his lip:
"Shh!"

    VII
After the endless jokes, this balmy winter
Around the pool, about the missing marbles,
What was more natural than for my birthday
To get — from the friend whose kiss that morning
    woke me —
A pregnantly clicking pouch of targets and strikers,
Aggies and rainbows, the opaque chalk-red ones,
Clear ones with DNA-like wisps inside,
Others like polar tempests vitrified . . .
These I've embedded at random in the deck slats

Around the pool. (The pool! — compact, blue, dancing,
Lit-from-beneath oubliette.) By night their sparkle
Repeats the garden lights, or moon- or starlight,
Tinily underfoot, as though the very
Here and now were becoming a kind of heaven
To sit in, talking, largely mindless of
The risen, cloudy brilliances above.

James Michie

 NINE TIMES

Nine times worse than abandonment by woman,
Because unappealable, because superhuman,
Is the scorn of the Muses — and rarely the wiser the poorer
Poet. Nine times, too, cooler than Nora
Walking out of her Doll's House of sham
With a flourish of doors is the quite soundless slam
With which inspiration leaves. Back jumps the Sahara,
Bringing the long-faced grasshoppers which are a
Burden, rubbing their legs and making grimaces,
Till paper becomes the parody of an oasis,
A patch of drought in a world of jeering garden.
God knows how those divine girls can harden
Their hearts against the old devoted beaux
Who fucked so boisterously once. God knows
How poetry greys insensibly to prose.

 DISCOVERER

White and curved as a shell she lies
On the long dune of the bed,

Mother-of-pearl in her nails and eyes;
    In her head
Oceanic themes have stirred
    Through leaning
Galleries sea-meaning
    Without foam of the word.

Who found the shell still hardly breathes
Lest he derange the music. Ear
Flattened against her body's wreaths
    To hear
The pulse of pleasure seized,
    He ponders
Over her name, and wonders
    At woman pleased.

Richard Moore

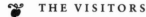 THE VISITORS

They like to come here. Pleasant sidestreets pave
        smoothly among the stones;
    a parking place at every grave;
a quiet suburb where the distant mower drones.

Instead of one they'd snarled at, he or she,
        or nagged with angry tears,
    the dirty, worn perplexity
they had endured at last in silence through the years,

    there is a polished stone and the mown grass
        over the buried dark;
    there is the shadow that will pass;
there are the muffled cars that glide and softly park.

Let there be no tears; let the easy plough
　　creature from creature sever.
　　Death is no inconvenience now.
At last no need for talking, talk all stopped forever.

Wasn't this peace, this clippered prettiness,
　　this silent presence here,
　　this still and sterilized caress,
what they had longed for always, always held most dear?

Frederick Morgan

 FEBRUARY 11, 1977

To my son John

You died nine years ago today.
I see you still sometimes in dreams
in white track-shirt and shorts, running,
against a drop of tropic green.

It seems to be a meadow, lying
open to early morning sun:
no other person is in view,
a quiet forest waits beyond.

Why do you hurry? What's the need?
Poor eager boy, why can't you see
once and for all you've lost this race
though you run for all eternity?

Your youngest brother's passed you by
at last: he's older now than you —

and all our lives have ramified
in meanings which you never knew.

And yet, your eyes still burn with joy,
your body's splendor never fades —
sometimes I seek to follow you
across the greenness, into the shade

of that great forest in whose depths
houses await and lives are lived,
where you haste in gleeful search of me
bearing a message I must have —

but I, before I change, must bide
the "days of my appointed time,"
and so I age from self to self
while you await me, always young.

Herbert Morris

 ### THE ROAD

I like the story of the circus waif
bought by the man-of-weights to be his mistress,
Profit the demon dragging her to market
and Lust the soul who paid in lire for her.

I like the peculiarities of her faith,
the startling quality of that innocence,
kissing the hand that dealt her cruelty
believing, poor and dumb, that this was love.

I relish a destitution stripped to sing
pure in a voice all passion and denial:

such are the driven burning by their breath
more than mere air allows and cold permits.

I savor my own involvement and concern
lest all the transformations seem unreal,
lest love be painted water-sweet and classic
rather than salt and anguish to the end.

I like her squatting in the village road
combing the dust for something of her own,
coming away belonging and committed,
roots to be cherished, stones she could befriend.

And what I like the subtlest and profoundest
is that the circus traveled grief to grief
educating the waif into a woman
loving and beautiful and fiercely proud.

I think of the sense of fury in that road,
stooping to scratch the earth out for a life
somewhere awaiting finding in one's name.
I like that, and I like the word Expense.

I think of the years together which they had,
the strong-man working her into the act,
that hint, despite himself, of some devotion.
I like that, and I like the ring of Cost.

Not in a root, or stone, but in a man
she found a thing to hold her tenderness.
I like her dedication after that,
her saying, if she spoke, I live by this.

And what I like pervasive and forever
is that my eyes have wept the tale before,
wanting the telling not so much as story
but for the way the waif befits my life.

Howard Moss

 MORNING GLORY

For Lee Krasner

Its wrinkled foreskin, twisting open, opens
The silky membrane of a French umbrella;
Within the lighted tent of the corolla
A five-ribbed shape (starfish invention!)
Supports, at the sun's behest, by tension
The small filament plumb at the center.

How blue is blue, how deft the manufacture
Of nature to define a color in a flower,
Balloon, trumpeter, and mountain climber
Among green hearts diagonally placed
In a matching, alternately rising pattern
On the overreaching wire of a stem

Always trying to ensnare another,
A string, anything, as long as it's above —
Chicken wire, trellis, fence rail, nail —
As if transcendence were simply a matter
Of going up and up, and up until
There's no place left in the world to go.

Andrew Motion

 WRITING

After what felt like a lifetime of rent
I bought somewhere my own. But at once,

in less than a week, he was writing:
Dear Madam, I hope you won't mind —

we met when I sold you the house.
It was mine. I gave you the china tea.
I showed you the room where you told me
yes, you could write in that room.

In the home I have now they are cruel.
There are traitors — and spies. I am hoping
my doctor is kind, but what is he doing
to bring me my wife, or give me her news?

Please, if this reaches you, tell her. Say —
if a visit is difficult, letters are fine.
Think of me reading this through at my desk,
throwing it down on my typewriter, frowning,

and wondering was this the room where she died?
Then think of my whisper to answer him:
Dearest heart. Forgive me. I'm ill
and dictating this. But I long for you always,

and when I'm recovered, I'll visit you.
Lazily spinning the phrases out, and finally
writing them, telling myself it was
kindness, and might even turn into love.

 THESE DAYS

It might be any night
these days, when every night
is like nothing on earth.
Tired with drinking, we long

for your riotous children
to wear themselves out
and shamble off to their beds.
Make it be soon, my eyes say

rolling up to the ceiling —
a relished, leisurely roll
which tells you as well
I want you. Bowing low

so your forehead rests
on the rumpled table-cloth
just for a second, you pour
milk in a shallow dish

for the cat, as he frisks in
out of nowhere, his hollow
lap-lap-lapping an almost
welcome distraction to stop me

pining for you, his tongue
steadily clearing the milk
like a tiny frog, revealing
a woman crossing a blue bridge

setting out on a journey,
perhaps, or coming back,
her parasol raised in salute,
her blue cross-hatched hat

tipped to deflect the wind,
and her eyes distinctly narrowed
to blue expressionless flecks
by a sudden onrush of light.

Paul Muldoon

 ### WHY BROWNLEE LEFT

Why Brownlee left, and where he went,
Is a mystery even now.
For if a man should have been content
It was him; two acres of barley,
One of potatoes, four bullocks,
A milker, a slated farmhouse.
He was last seen going out to plough
On a March morning, bright and early.

By noon Brownlee was famous;
They had found all abandoned, with
The last rig unbroken, his pair of black
Horses, like man and wife,
Shifting their weight from foot to
Foot, and gazing into the future.

Les A. Murray

 ### THE WIDOWER IN THE COUNTRY

I'll get up soon, and leave my bed unmade.
I'll go outside and split off kindling wood
from the yellow-box log that lies beside the gate,
and the sun will be high, for I get up late now.

I'll drive my axe in the log and come back in
with my armful of wood, and pause to look across
the Christmas paddocks aching in the heat,

the windless trees, the nettles in the yard . . .
and then I'll go in, boil water and make tea.

This afternoon, I'll stand out on the hill
and watch my house away below, and how
the roof reflects the sun and makes my eyes
water and close on bright webbed visions smeared
on the dark of my thoughts to dance and fade away.
Then the sun will move on, and I will simply watch,
or work, or sleep. And evening will come on.

Getting near dark, I'll go home, light the lamp
and eat my corned-beef supper, sitting there
at the head of the table. Then I'll go to bed.
Last night I thought I dreamed — but when I woke
the screaming was only a possum ski-ing down
the iron roof on little moonlit claws.

 SYDNEY AND THE BUSH

When Sydney and the Bush first met
there was no open ground
and men and girls, in chains and not,
all made an urgent sound.

Then convicts bled and warders bred,
the Bush went back and back,
the men of Fire and of Earth
became White men and Black.

When Sydney ordered lavish books
and warmed her feet with coal
the Bush came skylarking to town
and gave poor folk a soul.

Then bushmen sank and factories rose
and warders set the tone —

the Bush, in quarter-acre blocks,
helped families hold their own.

When Sydney and the Bush meet now
there is antipathy
and fashionable suburbs float
at night, far out to sea.

When Sydney rules without the Bush
she is a warders' shop
with heavy dancing overhead
the music will not stop

and when the drummers want a laugh
Australians are sent up.
When Sydney and the Bush meet now
there is no common ground.

Howard Nemerov

 INSOMNIA I

Some nights it's bound to be your best way out,
When nightmare is the short end of the stick,
When sleep is a part of town where it's not safe
To walk at night, when waking is the only way
You have of distancing your wretched dead,
A growing crowd, and escaping out of their
Time into yours for another little while;

Then pass ghostly, a planet in the house
Never observed, among the sleeping rooms
Where children dream themselves, and thence go down
Into the empty domain where daylight reigned;

Reward yourself with drink and a book to read,
A mystery, for its elusive gift
Of reassurance against the hour of death.
Order your heart about: *Stop doing that!*
And get the world to be secular again.

Then, when you know who done it, turn out the light,
And quietly in darkness, in moonlight, or snowlight
Reflective, listen to the whistling earth
In its backspin trajectory around the sun
That makes the planets sometimes retrograde
And brings the cold forgiveness of the dawn
Whose light extinguishes all stars but one.

THE MAKERS

Who can remember back to the first poets,
The greatest ones, greater even than Orpheus?
No one has remembered that far back
Or now considers, among the artifacts
And bones and cantilevered inference
The past is made of, those first and greatest poets,
So lofty and disdainful of renown
They left us not a name to know them by.

They were the ones that in whatever tongue
Worded the world, that were the first to say
Star, water, stone, that said the visible
And made it bring invisibles to view
In wind and time and change, and in the mind
Itself that minded the hitherto idiot world
And spoke the speechless world and sang the towers
Of the city into the astonished sky.

They were the first great listeners, attuned
To interval, relationship, and scale,

The first to say above, beneath, beyond,
Conjurors with love, death, sleep, with bread and wine,
Who having uttered vanished from the world
Leaving no memory but the marvelous
Magical elements, the breathing shapes
And stops of breath we build our Babels of.

THE WAR IN THE AIR

For a saving grace, we didn't see our dead,
Who rarely bothered coming home to die
But simply stayed away out there
In the clean war, the war in the air.

Seldom the ghosts came back bearing their tales
Of hitting the earth, the incompressible sea,
But stayed up there in the relative wind,
Shades fading in the mind,

Who had no graves but only epitaphs
Where never so many spoke for never so few:
Per ardua, said the partisans of Mars,
Per aspera, to the stars.

That was the good war, the war we won
As if there were no death, for goodness' sake,
With the help of the losers we left out there
In the air, in the empty air.

John Frederick Nims

 TIDE TURNING

Through salt marsh, grassy channel where the shark's
A rumor — lean, alongside — rides our boat;
Four of us off with picnic-things and wine.
Past tufty clutters of the mud called *pluff*,
Sun on the ocean tingles like a kiss.
About the fourth hour of the falling tide.

The six-hour-falling, six-hour-rising tide
Turns heron-haunts to alleys for the shark.
Tide-waters kiss and loosen; loosen, kiss.
Black-hooded terns blurt kazoo-talk — our boat
Now in midchannel and now rounding pluff.
Lolling, we eye the mud-tufts. Eye the wine.

The Atlantic, off there, dazzles. Who said wine-
Dark sea? Not this sea. Not at noon. The tide
Runs gold as chablis over sumps of pluff.
Too shallow here for lurkings of the shark,
His nose-cone, grin unsmiling. *Cr-ush!* the boat
Shocks, shudders — grounded. An abrupt tough kiss.

Our outboard's dug a mud-trough. Call that *kiss?*
Bronze knee bruised. A fair ankle gashed. With "wine-
Dark blood" a bard's on target here. The boat
Swivels, propeller in a pit, as tide
Withdraws in puddles round us — shows the shark-
Grey fin, grey flank, grey broadening humps of pluff.

Fingers that trailed in water, fume in pluff.
Wrist-deep, they learn how octopuses kiss.
Then — shark fins? No. Three dolphins there — *shhh!* — arc

Coquettish. As on TV. Cup of wine
To you, slaphappy sidekicks! with the tide's
Last hour a mudflat draining round the boat.

The hourglass turns. Look, tricklings toward the boat.
The first hour, poky, picks away at pluff.
The second, though, swirls currents. Then the tide's
Third, fourth — abundance! the great ocean's kiss.
The last two slacken. So? We're free, for wine
And gaudier mathematics. Toast the shark,

Good shark, a no-show. Glory floats our boat.
We, with the wine remaining — done with pluff —
Carouse on the affluent kisses of the tide.

Leslie Norris

 THE GIRLS OF LLANBADARN
(from the Welsh of Dafydd ap Gwilym)

Plague take them, every female!
With longing I'm bent double,
Yet not one of them, not one,
Is kind to my condition.
Golden girl, wise wife, harsh witch,
All reject my patronage.

What's their mischief, what malice
Makes them turn on me like this?
That one, with the fine eyebrows,
Can't she meet me in the trees?
There's no blame, no shame on her
To greet me in my green lair.

99

I have always been someone
So prodigal of passion
Not a single day goes by
But one or two catch my eye;
But here they all think of me
As some kind of enemy.
Every Sunday in Llanbadarn
There I'd be (no need to warn)
Bemused by some girl's beauty
(But my back to God's bounty)
And when I had ogled all,
Sweet-faced in seat or stall,
I'd hear one of them whisper
To the wise friend beside her:

"See that pale boy over there,
With his sister's long hair —
Don't trust him. Look at his eyes,
They're sly and lascivious."

"Is he like that? Then no chance,"
Says the friend, with a cold glance.
"He'll not get me, you may depend.
Let him roast till the world's end!"

What payment for my passion —
I've been sent to perdition.
I have to learn to restrain
My long pleasure in love's pain,
Must pack my bundles and flit,
A solitary hermit,
Must walk the world's cold boulder,
My head over my shoulder.
To look backwards, that's my fate,
A twisted neck, and no mate.

Robert Pinsky

 RALEGH'S PRIZES

And Summer turns her head with its dark tangle
All the way toward us; and the trees are heavy,
With little sprays of limp green maple and linden
Adhering after a rainstorm to the sidewalk
Where yellow pollen dries in pools and runnels.

Along the oceanfront, pink neon at dusk:
The long, late dusk, a light wind from the water
Lifting a girl's hair forward against her cheek
And swaying a chain of bulbs.
                                        In luminous booths,
The bright, traditional wheel is on its ratchet,
And ticking gaily at its little pawl;
And the surf revolves; and passing cars and people,
Their brilliant colors — all strange and hopeful as Ralegh's
Trophies: the balsam, the prizes of untried virtue,
Bananas and armadillos that a Captain
Carries his Monarch from another world.

Katha Pollitt

 OF THE SCYTHIANS

who came whirling out of the North
like a locust swarm, storm-darkening the sky,
their long hair whipping in the wind like the manes of horses,
no one remembers anything now but I:

how they screamed to the slaughter, as the skirl of a thousand
      flutes
fashioned from enemies' thighbones shrilled them on.
Naked they rode. We stood by our huts, stunned mute:
gold flashed from each spear, gold glittered on each arm.

I was a child in the temple. The old priest
hid me in a secret cellar with the images.
Above my head I heard him chant a last
prayer to the god. Since then

I scorn to mix with those who have come after.
Fat farmers, milky scribblers! What do they know
who have never heard the Scythians' terrible laughter
or seen in the wind their glittering wild hair flow?

 TWO FISH

Those speckled trout we glimpsed in a pool last year
you'd take for an image of love: it too should be
graceful, elusive, tacit, moving surely
among half-lights of mingled dim and clear,
forced to no course, of no fixed residence,
its only end its own swift elegance.
What would you say
if you saw what I saw the other day:
that pool heat-choked and fevered where sick blue
bubbled green scum and blistered water lily?
A white like a rolled-back eye or fish's belly
I thought I saw far out — but doubtless you
prefer to think our trout had left together
to seek a place with less inclement weather.

Christopher Reid

 THE GARDENERS

I love these gardens, all their show
of antiquated art nouveau:
the buxom ironwork, candle-drips
and blobby leafage.
        It is as if
someone had stumbled by surprise
on Alaodin's paradise.

It rains all evening — knives and forks.
The meteors drop by like corks.
Perpetuum mobile, a wind
hums in its box, as gardeners spend
endless, hermetic, twilight hours,
stooping above their hungry flowers.

This is the world's arcanest grove.
The borborygmus of a dove
calls from the belly of its bush.
How carefully the gardeners push
between the clumps of guzzling shrubs,
that line the way in wooden tubs.

With mashing faces, curled-up claws,
most of these blooms are carnivores.
Anyone sees, who wanders here,
a ruby clinging to an ear,
fat fingers, an outlandish wig . . .
The flowers grow slovenly and big,

as gardeners in white linen coats
rotate about their captious throats.

They have a god here, stern and jealous,
wearing four hats and five umbrellas,
who contemplates them, as they strive
to keep strange appetites alive.

Michael J. Rosen

 TOTAL ECLIPSE

The night of the eclipse we're parallel
in the unprecedented heat, secured
by just our fingers' intersecting touch.
Like the magician's other hand, the heat

distracts us while the moon vanishes
into the same black silk that conjures doves.
Making light of the heat, of anything
but the heat, we forget we meant to be up,

squinting to draw the moon into our lashes,
remarking how the blinds have magnified
the moon into a bright pinpoint of heat —
the moon! already half shadowed, half lit

on the window screen like a lunar moth.
So heavy-lidded, first one, then the other
detects some change: a quarter less, five-
eighths, or maybe still two halves . . .

we gaze until the moth closes its wings
and the same remaining crescent glistens
on your cheekbone, shoulder, hip — asleep
in a universe just outside my arms.

At 2:38, the scheduled fullest phase,
I wake you, once, though whether or not
you see the nothing that is there to see
— all overlapping shadows — I let you sleep.

For one held moment, the yielded space between us,
the unable-to-be-reasoned space beyond,
the sun and earth, my body, yours, the moon,
are all aligned in the predicted dark.

Gibbons Ruark

 LARKIN

This first-name-only business beggars history,
As if the young mistook Ben Jonson's need
To keep a certain name immaculate
Till darkness tugged his wrist in the graveyard road.

Nearsighted and too far off to wax familiar,
I would indulge the old formality
Of last names, since the man sank to his last hour
An ocean from my windows, low or high.

Larkin it is, then, with an added Philip
For those who would distinguish "English poet"
From, say, "Hero of the Dublin shipyards."
His road was a hero's byway, but he knew it.

Larkin I have been reading now since sunrise,
Or rather, with the day thus clouded over,
Morning. His trains on sidings, his racehorses
Nuzzling the dusk, his taking the measure

Of rainfall while we still look for a cloud,
His chosen solitude, a singular light
Dispensed by water in a lifted tumbler,
A real day's shouldered and delivered freight.

"This is not the full portion of whiskey,"
I muttered, young and tanked on Dylan Thomas,
But now his angle's undeniable.
Somebody, somewhere, is breaking a promise.

Surefooting through the rain of rice and horn-blare
Flattering some lovely daughter's wedding ride,
His tune is brassy, muted, grave, and just —
Jelly Roll's "Dead Man Blues" as the slow hearse glides.

Or think of it this way, as L for Larkin
Enters its cold-water flat in England's
Alphabet: Just now I was leaning forward,
His closed *High Windows* thin between my hands,

Palm to bare palm were it not for the poetry.
Knock in a nail and hang that image somewhere
Out of the way. Call it, should you think of it,
A man contemplating applause or prayer.

Carol Rumens

 VOCATION

Is it poetry I'm after at those moments when
I must clothe your hands in mine or comfort your shoulders
— so bare and neglected sometimes when we wake —
or press your mouth to taste its uncurling flower?

Is that which seems so fleshly and truthful merely
a twisted track into words, a way to leave you
for your image? Art is tempting, a colourful
infidelity with the self, and doubly feigning
when what is repossessed secretly by one
was made by two. And I wish I could pour a poetry-vodka
into twin glasses we'd gulp unanimously
("I poison myself for your health" the appropriate toast)
but only a poet would have acquired the taste
for such a strange distillation; you'd never warm
to heavy-petting dactyls, the squeak and creak
from locked, suburban stanzas. And so my fingers,
dancing alone, are less than content. They perceive
how they have clung to moral adolescence.
Their vocation now could be simply to talk to your skin,
to take you at kissing-time; later, to close your eyes
by stroking the lashes lightly over cheekbones
flushed with some high, bright, childish fever, and so
write the poem in the touch-shapes of darkness
and let it end there . . . They are on the tip of trusting
this silent, greyish room, its astonishing view
fading from metaphor to the life with you.

 IN THE CLOUD OF UNKNOWING

Goodbye, bright creature.
I would have had you
somewhere on solid earth,
wings clipped to pale

shoulder-blades,
and your fleecy head
a chrysanthemum, darkly
grown from my pillow.

I would have kept my tongue
for what salt weepings
it could tease from your finest
silences.

But it was written
into your book of life
that I should be brief.
Forbidden to count

the ways, denied
et cetera,
I worshipped the stone
from your supper-time plum,

the little hairs gleaned
in tears from the sheet.
Metaphysical desire
was all they would bear,

a bandage of art
for the low sob
of the vernacular,
a condition of prayer.

Now when I wake
and the dawn light names
your perfect absence,
I am at home,

lapped again
in my earliest language,
the vocatives tense
with desire and distance:

"Thou who art called
the Paraclete";

"After this our exile";
"Oh Sacred Heart!"

Dear iconoclast
forgive these texts
their cloudy haloes.
The intent pen burns

its slow path through
the slant rain of Greek,
the stars of Hebrew
. . . to touch your hem?

No, it was never
possible.
The old mystics knew
as they closed the book

on the dancing colours,
worn out with words
never made flesh
and with flesh that fought

their long abstraction.
They listened a moment;
the breath-soft foot-step
in the cloisters faded

as always to sighs;
the cold congress of leaves
in darkening autumn;
the wind's dissolution.

Mary Jo Salter

 ENGLAND

At times it seemed the country itself was a cloud
high up on the map, a sheepwool shape in the sea
that might as easily rise to break blue sky.
But meadows dipped beneath rough cows and horses;
rippled with short-fur grass, the scruff of earth.

As if, like me, they longed to come in early,
the cold days shrank from darkness.
I pedaled home uphill and saw the light
foreshorten, felt my beaded breath fall back.

Those mornings I would wake to watch the leaves rain.
Too damp to burn, their colors ran and blurred,
turning a mottled surface underneath.
Seeped in a world as kind as my intentions,
through miles of glass and cloud, I thought of you.

 WELCOME TO HIROSHIMA

is what you first see, stepping off the train:
a billboard brought to you in living English
by Toshiba Electric. While a channel
silent in the TV of the brain

projects those flickering re-runs of a cloud
that brims its risen columnful like beer
and, spilling over, hangs its foamy head,
you feel a thirst for history: what year

it started to be safe to breathe the air,
and when to drink the blood and scum afloat

on the Ohta River. But no, the water's clear,
they pour it for your morning cup of tea

in one of the countless sunny coffee shops
whose plastic dioramas advertise
mutations of cuisine behind the glass:
a pancake sandwich; a pizza someone tops

with a maraschino cherry. Passing by
the Peace Park's floral hypocenter (where
how bravely, or with what mistaken cheer,
humanity erased its own erasure),

you enter the memorial museum
and through more glass are served, as on a dish
of blistered grass, three mannequins. Like gloves
a mother clips to coatsleeves, strings of flesh

hang from their fingertips; or as if tied
to recall a duty for us, *Reverence
the dead whose mourners too shall soon be dead,*
but all commemoration's swallowed up

in questions of bad taste, how re-created
horror mocks the grim original,
and thinking at last *They should have left it all*
you stop. This is the wristwatch of a child.

Jammed on the moment's impact, resolute
to communicate some message, although mute,
it gestures with its hands at eight-fifteen
and eight-fifteen and eight-fifteen again

while tables of statistics on the wall
update the news by calling on a roll
of tape, death gummed on death, and in the case
adjacent, an exhibit under glass

is glass itself: a shard the bomb slammed in
a woman's arm at eight-fifteen, but some
three decades on — as if to make it plain
hope's only as renewable as pain,

and as if all the unsung
debasements of the past may one day come
rising to the surface once again —
worked its filthy way out like a tongue.

Gjertrud Schnackenberg

 ### SUPERNATURAL LOVE

My father at the dictionary-stand
Touches the page to fully understand
The lamplit answer, tilting in his hand

His slowly scanning magnifying lens,
A blurry, glistening circle he suspends
Above the word "Carnation." Then he bends

So near his eyes are magnified and blurred,
One finger on the miniature word,
As if he touched a single key and heard

A distant, plucked, infinitesimal string,
"The obligation due to every thing
That's smaller than the universe." I bring

My sewing needle close enough that I
Can watch my father through the needle's eye,
As through a lens ground for a butterfly

Who peers down flower-hallways toward a room
Shadowed and fathomed as this study's gloom
Where, as a scholar bends above a tomb

To read what's buried there, he bends to pore
Over the Latin blossom. I am four,
I spill my pins and needles on the floor

Trying to stitch "Beloved" X by X.
My dangerous, bright needle's point connects
Myself illiterate to this perfect text

I cannot read. My father puzzles why
It is my habit to identify
Carnations as "Christ's flowers," knowing I

Can give no explanation but "Because."
Word-roots blossom in speechless messages
The way the thread behind my sampler does

Where following each X I awkward move
My needle through the word whose root is love.
He reads, "A pink variety of Clove,

Carnatio, the Latin, meaning flesh."
As if the bud's essential oils brush
Christ's fragrance through the room, the iron-fresh

Odor carnations have floats up to me,
A drifted, secret, bitter ecstasy,
The stems squeak in my scissors, *Child, it's me,*

He turns the page to "Clove" and reads aloud:
"The clove, a spice, dried from a flower-bud."
Then twice, as if he hasn't understood,

He reads, "From French, for *clou,* meaning a nail."
He gazes, motionless. "Meaning a nail."
The incarnation blossoms, flesh and nail,

I twist my threads like stems into a knot
And smooth "Beloved," but my needle caught
Within the threads, *Thy blood so dearly bought,*

The needle strikes my finger to the bone.
I lift my hand, it is myself I've sewn,
The flesh laid bare, the threads of blood my own,

I lift my hand in startled agony
And call upon his name, "Daddy daddy" —
My father's hand touches the injury

As lightly as he touched the page before,
Where incarnation bloomed from roots that bore
The flowers I called Christ's when I was four.

Alan Shapiro

 FAMILIAR STORY

Tonight they need to be both host and stranger,
talking together all evening after dinner;
the candle wavering down till they are half
in darkness as they lead each other back
through their accumulated separate lore,
telling the stories they have told before
to other lovers, who are stories now.
They give no truth here, but the practised glow
of truthfulness: even as they confess
wholeheartedly to niggling attentiveness

disguised as love, to no or too much care,
affection parceled out till it's not there —
the more one tells, the more the other sees
just how appealing is this honesty,
how generous they are to those who hurt them.
They think this kind shrewd vision won't desert them.
And tonight, at least, it won't as they forget
what all their lore will lead them to expect
of one another, what they'll later owe
day after each slow day when all they know
is the familiar story they are living,
restless, and remote, and unforgiving.
It's then, when they don't feel it, they will need
the love bad days require and impede.
But not tonight, the candle going, gone,
their eyes shut briefly as the light goes on.
Tonight desire is generosity,
desire in each other's all they see,
and all else now is no more than the light
hurting their eyes, too sudden and too bright.

L. E. Sissman

 COCKAIGNE: A DREAM

> CHORUS OF ALL: Then our Age was in it's Prime,
> Free from Rage, and free from Crime,
> A very Merry, Dancing, Drinking,
> Laughing, Quaffing, and unthinking Time.
> (*Dance of Diana's Attendants. Enter Mars.*)
> — *"The Secular Masque,"* by John Dryden

Coming around the corner of the dream
City I've lived in nights since I was ten —
Amalgamated of a lost New York,

A dead Detroit, a trussed and mummified
Skylineless Boston with a hint thrown in
Of Philadelphia and London in
An early age, all folded into a
Receipt (or a lost pawn slip) for a place
That tasted of a human sweetness, laced
With grandeur and improbability —
I passed the old cast-iron hotel where I
Had sat and talked and sipped a cheap cognac
In many a dream, and came out on the fore-
Side of a wide white river promenade
Crossed by a dun-green "L" stark overhead
And paralleled, across the river, by
Another larger elevated steel
Conception of sequoia girders — a
Throg's Neck usurping all the western air
And staining it its brighter green. The east
Bank, though, was still its unprogressed,
Arrested older self. To learn the time,
I detoured down an alleyway between
Two ranks of small, chapfallen shops, and off
A rusty paper rack chained to the steps
Of a moribund grocerette I bought — five cents —
A copy of the Boston *Morning Globe*
For April 7th, 1953.
Northbound again upon the promenade,
I caught an air of spring, a clef or key
Of untuned song, a snatch of melody
In untrained voices carrying no tune
But the light burden of the first warm day
Set loose, light-headed, in the open, to
Salute the single minute of the year
When all's forgiven life, the garroter
Who still stands sentry on the darkening stair
In every stifling rooming house. Alone,
But only literally, I proceed
Past faces that have all the love they need

For once, and can, for once, give some away,
As their smiles give away, their eyes betray,
Level, for once, with mine, and not cast down.
A great glass café, half a riverboat,
Half Crystal Palace, beckons; I step in
To ranks of white enamel tables, wire,
Wood-seated ice-cream-parlor chairs,
And, in the place of honor by the door,
A towering cardboard mockup, like a cake
Of a French battleship, the *Richelieu,*
Around which sailors cluster, jabbering
In French, which figures, since the French fleet's in.
Uproom, in the glass-ceilinged, vasty hall,
Quite like a Continental station, all
The places have been set at an oblong
Long banquet table. As I approach it, all
My dearest friends, looking, in 1953,
Precisely as, in fact, they look today,
Rise from some ambush and, laughing, welcome me
To the fraternal order of the spring.
A pause; an unheard drum roll; from the other side
Of the table steps forth, smiling, Anne, my wife,
And I awaken at twelve-fifty-five
A.M., according to the bedside clock,
On February 14th of this year,
Elated, desolate it could not spell
Me any longer, being but a dream,
Its only evidence being my tears
Of joy or of the other, I can't tell.

DECEMBER 27, 1966

Night sweat: my temperature spikes to 102
At 5 A.M. — a classic symptom — and,
Awake and shaken by an ague, I
Peep out a western window at the worn

Half-dollar of the moon, couched in the rose
And purple medium of air above
The little, distant mountains, a black line
Of gentle ox humps, flanked by greeny lights
Where a still empty highway goes. In Christmas week,
The stars flash ornamentally with the
Pure come-on of a possibility
Of peace beyond all reason, of the spheres
Engaged in an adagio saraband
Of perfect mathematic to set an
Example for the earthly, who abide
In vales of breakdown out of warranty,
The unrepairable complaint that rattles us
To death. Tonight, though, it is almost worth the price —
High stakes, and the veiled dealer vends bad cards —
To see the moon so silver going west,
So ladily serene because so dead,
So closely tailed by her consort of stars,
So far above the feverish, shivering
Nightwatchman pressed against the falling glass.

C. H. Sisson

 BLACK ROCKS

And those Black Rocks which overhung the stream
Remain still sturdily within my dream.
Black Rocks in summer! when the river rides
By them like muddy sea on shallow tides,
Yet lively where the ripples hump and blink.
Dark-surfaced stone had dried like Indian ink

But trees were darker where they stretched across
Like staring cranes, and to its certain loss
The mind crept out on branches without hold.

I can explain those mornings, fishing net
Firm in my grasp, but I have nothing yet,
An empty jam-jar swinging from a string,
The home to breakfast and that other thing
More dreaded than a stranger and more cruel,
The over-shadow of a day at school.
Where, when I come, and once within the gate,
No use of language, hardly am I here
Except to register the scale of fear
— An exile from the world of flesh and bone,
The prisoner of minds and walls of stone.

William Jay Smith

 JOURNEY TO THE INTERIOR

He has gone into the forest,
to the wooded mind in wrath;
he will follow out the nettles
and the bindweed path.

He is torn by tangled roots,
he is trapped by mildewed air;
he will feed on alder shoots
and on fungi: in despair

he will pursue each dry creek-bed,
each hot white gully's rough raw stone

till heaven opens overhead
a vast jawbone

and trees around grow toothpick-thin
and a deepening dustcloud swirls about
and every road leads on within
and none leads out.

BACHELOR'S-BUTTONS

Bachelor's-buttons are fine to see
When one is unattached and free,

When days are long and cares are few
And every green field sown with blue

Cornflowers that profusely seem
Attendant on a young man's dream.

Bachelor's-buttons are fine to see
When one knows no frugality;

And splendid to behold again
Lacing a jacket of gold grain,

A border tended by a wife
Who mends the fraying edge of life;

Who fashions in a hundred ways
Bright seams that cut through one's dark days;

Or will until buttons are counted and sold,
And the blue thread breaks, and earth is cold.

W. D. Snodgrass

 MUTABILITY

It was all different; that, at least, seemed sure.
We still agreed — but only that she'd changed.
Some things that you still loved might still endure.

You woke in your own, big, dove-tailed bed, secure
And warm — but the whole room felt rearranged.
It was all different; that, at least, seemed sure.

The lamp stood four-square — like your furniture;
The air'd gone tinged, though, or the light deranged.
Some things that you still loved might still endure

Outside. Your fields stretched, a parched upland moor
Where shadows paired and split, where lean shapes ranged.
It was all different; that, at least, seemed sure

And that, from here on in, you could count on fewer
Second chances. Some rules might be arranged;
Some things that you still loved might still endure,

Though some old friends would close, soon, for the pure
Joy of the kill — no prisoners exchanged.
It was all different; that, at least, seemed sure.

Maybe the injuries weren't past all cure.
No luck lasts; yours might not, too long, stay estranged;
Some things that you still loved might still endure.
It was all different; that, at least, seemed sure.

Elizabeth Spires

 TWO SHADOWS

For Madison

When we are shadows watching over shadows,
when years have passed, enough to live
two lives, when we have passed
through love and come out speechless
on the other side, I will remember
how we spent a night, walking the streets
                          in August, side by side,
following two shadows dressed in long gray coats,
unseasonable clothes they didn't seem to mind,
walking so easily, with easy stride,
merging for a moment, then isolate,
as they led us to your street, your door,
and up the steps until, inside,
love became articulate: eye, lip, and brow.
When we are shadows watching over shadows,
we will not speak of it but *know,* and turn
again toward each other tenderly,
                          shadow to shadow.

 0°

These nights when the wind blows,
I lay my head on the pillow,
I lay my head on white feathers,
white down, tag ends of Memory.
White feathers, white down,
I'm wrapped in a nightgown stiffening,
year by year, against the cold.

My arms hug the pillow, light
as a feather when we lie in love's
weather, but tonight I sleep alone,
the closet full of skeletons that grin
in the chilly breeze. Starving,
they climb love's zero by degrees,
as I will, the pillow dreaming
furious dreams. Dreams not my own.

Timothy Steele

 THE SHEETS

From breezeway or through front porch screen
You'd see the sheets, wide blocks of white
Defined against a backdrop of
A field whose grasses were a green
    Intensity of light.

How fresh they looked there on the line,
Their laundered sweetness through the hours
Gathering richly in the air
While cumulus clouds gathered in
    Topheavily piled towers.

We children tightroped the low walls
Along the garden; bush and bough
And the washed sheets moved in the wind;
And thinking of this now recalls
    Vasari's tale of how

Young Leonardo, charmed of sight,
Would buy in the loud marketplace

Caged birds and set them free — thus yielding
Back to the air which gave him light
    Lost beauty and lost grace.

So with the sheets: for as they drew
Clear warming sunlight from the sky,
They gave to light their rich, clean scent.
And when, the long day nearly through,
    My cousin Anne and I

Would take the sheets down from the line,
We'd fold in baskets their crisp heat,
Absorbing, as they had, the fine
Steady exchange of earth and sky,
    Material and sweet.

AURORA

Your sleep is so profound
This room seems a recess
Awaiting consciousness.
Gauze curtains, drawn around
The postered bed, confute
Each waking attribute —
Volition, movement, sound.

Outside, though, chilly light
Shivers a puddle's coil
Of iridescent oil;
Windows, sun-struck, ignite;
Doves strut along the edge
Of roof- and terrace-ledge
And drop off into flight.

And soon enough you'll rise.
Long-gowned and self-aware,

Brushing life through your hair,
You'll notice with surprise
The way your glass displays,
Twin-miniatured, your face
In your reflective eyes.

Goddess, it's you in whom
Our clear hearts joy and chafe.
Awaken, then. Vouchsafe
Ideas to resume.
Draw back the drapes: let this
Quick muffled emphasis
Flood light across the room.

Anne Stevenson

 THE PRICE

The fear of loneliness, the wish
to be alone;
love grown rank as seeding grass
in every room,
and anger at it, raging at it,
storming it down.

Also that four-walled chrysalis
and impediment, home;
that lamp and hearth, that easy fit
of bed to bone;
those children, too, sharp witnesses
of all I've done.

My dear, the ropes that bind us
are safe to hold;

the walls that crush us keep us
from the cold.
I know the price and still I pay it, pay it —
words, their furtive kiss,
illicit gold.

THE FICTION-MAKERS

We were the wrecked elect,
the ruined few. Youth,
youth, the Café Iruña
and the bullfight set,
looped on Lepanto brandy
but talking "truth" —
Hem, the 4 A.M. wisecrack,
the hard way in,
that story we were all at the end of
and couldn't begin —
we thought we were living now,
but we were living then.

Sanctified Pound, a knot
of nerves in his fist,
squeezing the Goddamn iamb
out of our verse,
making it new in his
archaeological plot —
to maintain "the sublime"
in the factive? Couldn't be done.
Something went wrong
with "new" in the Pisan pen.
He thought he was making now,
but he was making then.

Virginia, Vanessa,
a teapot, a Fitzroy fuss,

"Semen?" asks Lytton,
eyeing a smudge on a dress.
How to educate England
and keep a correct address
on the path to the river through
Auschwitz? Belsen?
Auden and Isherwood
stalking glad boys in Berlin —
they thought they were suffering now,
but they were suffering then.

Out of pink-cheeked Cwmdonkin,
Dylan with his Soho grin.
Planted in the fiercest of flames,
gold ash on a stem.
When Henry jumped out of his joke,
Mr Bones sat in.
Even you, with your breakable heart
in your ruined skin,
those poems all written
that have to be you, dear friend,
you guessed you were dying now,
but you were dying then.

Here is a table with glasses,
ribbed cages tipped back,
or turned on a hinge to each other
to talk, to talk,
mouths that are drinking or smiling
or quoting some book,
or laughing out laughter as candletongues
lick at the dark —
so bright in this fiction
forever becoming its end,
we think we are laughing now,
but we are laughing then.

❦ MAKING POETRY

"You have to inhabit poetry
if you want to make it."

And what's "to inhabit"?

To be in the habit of, to wear
words, sitting in the plainest light,
in the silk of morning, in the shoe of night;
a feeling, bare and frondish in surprising air;
familiar . . . rare.

And what's "to make"?

To be and to become words' passing
weather; to serve a girl on terrible
terms, embark on voyages over voices,
evade the ego-hill, the misery-well,
the siren hiss of *publish, success, publish,
success, success, success.*

And why inhabit, make, inherit poetry?

Oh, it's the shared comedy of the worst
blessed; the sound leading the hand;
a wordlife running from mind to mind
through the washed rooms of the simple senses;
one of those haunted, undefendable, unpoetic
crosses we have to find.

May Swenson

 MORNING AT POINT DUME

Blond stones all round-sided,
that the tide has tumbled on sand's table,
like large warm loaves strewn in the sun.

Wet pathways drain among them, sandgrains
diamond in morning light.
A high-hipped dog trots toward the sea,

followed by a girl, naked, young,
breasts jouncing, and long fair hair.
Girl and dog in the hissing surf

roister, dive and swim together,
bodies flashing dolphin-smooth,
the hair in her delta crisp dark gold.

The Pacific is cold. Rushed ashore on a wave,
her body blushes with stings of spume.
Running upslope, the circling dog

leaps to her hand, scatters spray
from his thick blond malamute fur.
Together they twine the stone loaves' maze.

Girl lets her glistening belly down
on a yellow towel on hard hot sand,
dog panting, *couchant* by her side.

Five surfers in skintight black
rubber suits, their plexiglass
boards on shoulders, stride the shore,

their eyes searching the lustrous water
for the hills of combers that build far out,
to mount and ride the curling snowtops.

The sunburned boys in phalanx pass,
squinting ahead, scuffing sand.
Without a glance at the yellow towel

they advance to the sea.
Enormous breakers thunder in.
Falling, they shake the ground.

Anthony Thwaite

 SIMPLE POEM

I shall make it simple so you understand.
Making it simple will make it clear for me.
When you have read it, take me by the hand
As children do, loving simplicity.

This is the simple poem I have made.
Tell me you understand. But when you do
Don't ask me in return if I have said
All that I meant, or whether it is true.

 DREAM TIME

Waking from a bad dream, and thrashing out
So that you too woke, and I heard you say
"What is it, love?" — why, at my sudden shout,
Did I pretend more stirs, more mutterings,

A kind of baleful play,
And knew I left you with sad wonderings?

Was it because the dream that made me speak
Excluded you, close though you were to me
And are? For each one's dreaming is unique:
Rejected here and there we lie alone,
Separate, distinct, free,
Each one's heart as heavy as a stone.

Charles Tomlinson

 RHYMES

Perfect is the word I can never hear
    Without a sensation as of seeing —
As though a place should grow perfectly clear,
    The light on the look of it agreeing
To show — not all there is to be seen,
    But all you would wish to know
At a given time. Word and world rhyme
    As the penstrokes might if you drew
The spaciousness reaching down through a valley view,
    Gathering the lines into its distances
As if they were streams, as if they were eye-beams:
    Perfect, then, the eye's command in its riding,
Perfect the coping hand, the hillslopes
    Drawing it into such sight the sight would miss,
Guiding the glance the way perfection is.

❦ THE SHAFT

For Guy Davenport

The shaft seemed like a place of sacrifice:
    You climbed where spoil heaps from the hill
Spilled out into a wood, the slate
    Tinkling underfoot like shards, and then
You bent to enter: a passageway:
    Cervix of stone: the tick of waterdrops,
A clear clepsydra: and squeezing through
    Emerged into cathedral space, held-up
By a single rocksheaf, a gerbe
    Buttressing-back the roof. The shaft
Opened beneath it, all its levels
    Lost in a hundred feet of water.
Those miners — dust, beards, mattocks —
    They photographed seventy years ago,
Might well have gone to ground here, pharaohs
    Awaiting excavation, their drowned equipment
Laid-out beside them. All you could see
    Was rock reflections tunneling the floor
That water covered, a vertical unfathomed,
    A vertigo that dropped through centuries
To the first who broke into these fells:
    The shaft was not a place to stare into
Or not for long: the adit you entered by
    Filtered a leaf-light, a phosphorescence,
Doubled by water to a tremulous fire
    And signalling you back to the moist door
Into whose darkness you had turned aside
    Out of the sun of an unfinished summer.

David Wagoner

 MY FATHER'S GARDEN

On his way to the open hearth where white-hot steel
Boiled against furnace walls in wait for his lance
To pierce the fireclay and set loose demons
And dragons in molten tons, blazing
Down to the huge satanic caldrons,
Each day he would pass the scrapyard, his kind of garden.

In rusty rockeries of stoves and brake drums,
In grottoes of sewing machines and refrigerators,
He would pick flowers for us: small gears and cogwheels
With teeth like petals, with holes for anthers,
Long stalks of lead to be poured into toy soldiers,
Ball bearings as big as grapes to knock them down.

He was called a melter. He tried to keep his brain
From melting in those tyger-mouthed mills
Where the same steel reappeared over and over
To be reborn in the fire as something better
Or worse: cannons or cars, needles or girders,
Flagpoles, swords, or plowshares.

But it melted. His classical learning ran
Down and away from him, not burning bright.
His fingers culled a few cold scraps of Latin
And Greek, *magna sine laude,* for crosswords
And brought home lumps of tin and sewer grills
As if they were his ripe prize vegetables.

🌳 ON MOTEL WALLS

Beyond the foot of the bed: a seascape whose ocean,
Under the pummeling of a moon the shape and shade
Of a wrecking ball, is breaking into slabs
Against a concrete coast. Next to the closet:
A landscape of pasty mountains no one could climb
Or fall from, beyond whose sugary grandeur
Lies Flatland, a blankness plastered on plasterboard.
And over the bed: a garden in the glare
Of shadowless noon where flowerheads burst more briefly
And emptily and finally than fireworks.

For hours, I've been a castaway on that shore
By that fake water where nothing was ever born,
Where the goddess of beauty sank. I've flopped on those
        slopes
Where no one on earth could catch a breath worth breathing,
And I've been caught in that garden
Where the light is neither waves nor particles
But an inorganic splatter without a source.

Tonight, what's in the eye of this beholder
Is less and less and all the ways I can go
Dead wrong myself through the quick passing
Of sentences: tomorrow, I may be staring
Straight in the face of the hanging judge of my future
Who'll read me with the deadpan of a jailer
Before a search, a lock-down, and lights out.
I'll do hard time all night inside these walls
In my mind's eye, a transient facing a door
That says, *Have you forgotten anything
Of value? Have you left anything behind?*

Jeffrey Wainwright

 THE FIERCE DREAM

I dreamt last night
A fierce dream
Of a tree
That in my garden grew,
But the garden became
A burying ground,
From the graves sleek flowers drew.

The summer so
Encased the air
It seemed we moved
In a golden bell.
But all the time
From the springing tree
The leaves and blossoms fell.

The blossom I caught
In a yellow jug,
But that then slipped my hand —
Upon the flag below
A single sound.
Pearls and red drops
From all the fragments flow.

A dream so struck
From ragged sleep
Sucks out the redness
From the day.
The mind swoons to see again
How it contrives
Its own dismay.

ILLUMINATION

That is her lover lying there,
And she beside him lying close.
They do not speak, or move, or touch.
The lucid grass between them flows.

To lie, in stillness, breathing just,
Might motion time towards desire.
The air now barely moves the grass.
The sun in white draws off its fire.

Derek Walcott

 THE YOUNG WIFE

For Nigel

Make all your sorrow neat.
Plump pillows, soothe the corners
of her favourite coverlet.
Write to her mourners.

At dusk, after the office,
travel an armchair's ridge,
the valley of the shadow in the sofas,
the drapes' dead foliage.

Ah, but the mirror — the mirror
which you believe has seen
the traitor you feel you are —
clouds, though you wipe it clean!

The buds on the wallpaper
do not shake at the muffled sobbing

the children must not hear,
or the drawers you dare not open.

She has gone with that visitor
that sat beside her, like wind
clicking shut the bedroom door;
arm in arm they went,

leaving her wedding photograph in
its lace frame, a face smiling at
itself. And the telephone
without a voice. The weight

we bear on this heavier side
of the grave brings no comfort.
But the vow that was said
in white lace has brought

you now to the very edge
of that promise; now, for some,
the hooks in the hawthorn hedge
break happily into blossom

and the heart into grief.
The sun slants on a kitchen floor.
You keep setting a fork and knife
at her place for supper.

The children close in the space
made by a chair removed,
and nothing takes her place,
loved and now deeper loved.

The children accept your answer.
They startle you when they laugh.
She sits there smiling that cancer
kills everything but Love.

Robert Penn Warren

 ## WHAT VOICE AT MOTH-HOUR

What voice at moth-hour did I hear calling
As I stood in the orchard while the white
Petals of apple blossoms were falling,
Whiter than moth-wing in that twilight?

What voice did I hear as I stood by the stream,
Bemused in the murmurous wisdom there uttered,
While ripples at stone, in their steely gleam,
Caught last light before it was shuttered?

What voice did I hear as I wandered alone
In a premature night of cedar, beech, oak,
Each foot set soft, then still as stone
Standing to wait while the first owl spoke?

The voice that I heard once at dew-fall, I now
Can hear by a simple trick. If I close
My eyes, in that dusk I again know
The feel of damp grass between bare toes,

Can see the last zigzag, sky-skittering, high,
Of a bullbat, and even hear, far off, from
Swamp-cover, the whip-o-will, and as I
Once heard, hear the voice: *It's late! Come home.*

 ## HISTORY DURING NOCTURNAL SNOWFALL

Dark in the cubicle boxed from snow-darkness of night,
Where that soundless paradox summarizes the world,
We lie, each alone, and I reach a finger laid light
To a wrist that does not move, as I think of a body curled —

Is it an inch, or a world, away — a watch-tick
Or a century off? In darkness I compress my eyes
And wonder if I might devise the clever trick
Of making heartbeat with heartbeat synchronize.

Each has come a long way to this wordless and windless
       burrow,
Each, like a mole, clawing blindly, year after year,
Each clawing and clawing through blindness of joy and
       sorrow,
And neither knowing how the world outside might appear.

Could one guess the other's buried narrative?
How the other, in weal or woe, might have found
White darkness where, a finger on wrist, one might live
In the synchronized rhythm of heart, and heart, with no sound?

Was it a matter of chance? Or miracle?
Or which is which — for logic laughs at both?
Could it matter less as whiteness and darkness blending fall
And my finger touches a pulse to intuit its truth.

LAST MEETING

A Saturday night in August when
Farm folks and tenants and black farmhands
Used to crowd the street of a market town
To do their "traden," and chew the rag,

And to hide the likker from women hung out
Behind the poolroom or barbershop —
If you were white. If black, in an alley.
And the odor of whiskey mixed with the sweat

And cheap perfume, and high heels waggled
On worn bricks, and through the crowd

I saw her come. I see her now
As plain as then — some forty years back.

It's like a flash, and still she comes,
Comes peering at me, not sure yet,
For I'm in my city clothes and hat,
But in the same instant we recognize

Each other. I see the shrunken old woman
With bleary eyes and yellow-gray skin,
And walking now with the help of a stick.
We hug and kiss there in the street.

"Ro-Penn, Ro-Penn, my little tadpole,"
She said, and patted my cheek, and said,
"Git off yore hat so I'll see yore haid."
And I did. She ran her hands through thinning hair.

"Not fahr-red, like it used to be."
And ran her fingers some more. "And thinner,
And sandy color some places too."
Then she rocked her arms like cuddling a child,

And crooned, and said, "Now big and gone
Out in the wide world — but 'member me!"
I tried to say "I couldn't forget,"
But the words wouldn't come, and I felt how frail

Were the vertebrae I clasped. I felt
Tears run down beside her nose,
And a crazy voice, like some half-laugh,
Said, "Chile, yore Ma's dead, yore Pappy ole,

"But I'm hangen on fer what I'm wuth."
So we said goodbye, with eyes staring at us
And laughter in some corner, somewhere.
That was the last time we ever met.

All's changed. The faces on the street
Are changed. I'm rarely back. But once
I tried to find her grave, and failed.
Next time I'll promise adequate time.

And find it. I might take store-bought flowers
(Though not a florist in twenty miles),
But a fruit jar full of local zinnias
Might look even better with jimson weed.

It's nigh half a lifetime I haven't managed,
But there must be enough time left for that.

Rosanna Warren

 HISTORY AS DECORATION

Float over us, Florence, your banners
of assassination, your most expensive
reds: Brazil, Majorca lichen, cochineal.
Let the Neoplatonic Arno flow
crocus yellow. Let palazzo walls
flaunt quattrocento dyes: "little
monk" and "lion skin." We pay for beauty; beautiful
are gorgeous crimes we cannot feel —

they shone so long ago. And those philosophies
too pretty in spirit ever to be real.
City of fashion. Leonardo chose
the hanged Pazzi conspirator for a theme:
"Tawny cap; black satin vest," he wrote,
"black sleeveless coat, lined; turquoise
jacket lined with fox; Bernardo di
Bandino Baroncigli; black hose."

So dangled the elegant corpse, *bella figura*
though its tongue stuck out. The keen, gossipy
faces still peer from Ghirlandaio's walls
and from the streets we elbow through today.
History flashes in banknotes. Gold, jade, corals
twinkle from hand to hand, while the spectral glare
of Savonarola's sunset bonfire licks the square
and his cries ascend and blend with Vespers bells.

❧ TO MAX JACOB

You *were* a moral dandy, sir. The font
could have twinkled with eau-de-cologne
for all you cared; the point
was only the soul's toilette, to keep
malicious Max immaculate. The stone
on which you knelt was bare,
the walls you prayed to innocent
of any devil's ornament. And yet
your piety is touching, though
(because?) histrionic: grown
old with the actor, the gesture must
approach perfection of artifice.
Superbly you litter your skull with dust,
raise up trembling lips to kiss
the godly Host. You've scarce a hair
but yank what you can, by God,
right out at the roots.
A fourteen-year scenario
of Job on ash heap, vile,
repentant, all the while
so deadly bored you write your friends,
"The quality of work depends
all, on the *kind* of boredom."
What interior desert did you fear

so terribly, you chose
a monk's cell, not the city, for your stage?
And for your major prop, the rose
of Christ, and not of Baudelaire?

Theodore Weiss

 ANOTHER AND ANOTHER AND . . .

. . . to go on living after all.
— *Odysseus*

Even the liveliest of us had
to regale himself with farfetched
lives he had not lived, spontaneous
roles, spun out with plots, inspired
complications, accidents, seafaring,
like the spumy wonders that his wife
aggrandized daily from her hands.

It must have refreshed him
for a moment to shed his briny,
pounded body, habits of a lifetime,
tugging always, nagging at him,
like the gods, fate he must follow,
for its daily due, allowing never
one digression from its course.

But given the space, a new
world waiting — charged though
it might be with trials, dangers —
of a stranger's eyes and ears,
stage like no other to frisk on,

apt for any fantastical performance,
he could assume a mask, that role
lighter than feathers with wings

working them: a name, names
made of breath alone, and deeds
to stroll in like a god, the same
daring, the same freedom. And those
eyes, sparkling their amazement,
mounted snowy peaks upon his words,
composed — those ears — a music balmy
round him birds might loll in,

glad to add, to drown in,
their own most luxuriant songs.
For a moment, far past all that he
had done, was yet in ways unknown
to him to do, he was free to wander
the way — lighthearted, true — of his
own wish, to do the things he was
not meant to. And by feigning so,

his acting another and another and . . . ,
he became that much more himself.

From EVERY SECOND THOUGHT

And thence return me to my Milan, where
Every third thought shall be my grave.
— *Prospero*

A grey and dankish thing
this day, here in the winter
of your years, each blustering
winter all year long.
                                        Gusts

peevish at you, mutterings,
you huddle by the fitful fire.
Light — just enough
                    for dark
to score itself, a riches much
too packed to be spelled out —
flips woods,
              one instant
gold and green, sky shooting
fire-caps that crest a mild,
swart sea.
            But, shivering,
do you not regret their loss,
those powers you thought able
to ensnare the world
                      in song?
In your regardless corner-shade
you drowse: the hours pass
remarkable
              as random clouds.
Yet clouds, building at a glance,
once cobbled sky a causeway
nymphs and deities
                    traversed.
Who now attends, amazed to think
this dried grey stalk, young,
crowned itself
                with flowers?

Richard Wilbur

 LYING

To claim, at a dead party, to have spotted a grackle,
When in fact you haven't of late, can do no harm.
Your reputation for saying things of interest
Will not be marred, if you hasten to other topics,
Nor will the delicate web of human trust
Be ruptured by that airy fabrication.
Later, however, talking with toxic zest
Of golf, or taxes, or the rest of it
Where the beaked ladle plies the chuckling ice,
You may enjoy a chill of severance, hearing
Above your head the shrug of unreal wings.
Not that the world is tiresome in itself:
We know what boredom is: it is a dull
Impatience or a fierce velleity,
A champing wish, stalled by our lassitude,
To make or do. In the strict sense, of course,
We invent nothing, merely bearing witness
To what each morning brings again to light:
Gold crosses, cornices, astonishment
Of panes, the turbine-vent which natural law
Spins on the grill-end of the diner's roof,
Then grass and grackles or, at the end of town
In sheen-swept pastureland, the horse's neck
Clothed with its usual thunder, and the stones
Beginning now to tug their shadows in
And track the air with glitter. All these things
Are there before us; there before we look
Or fail to look; there to be seen or not
By us, as by the bee's twelve thousand eyes,
According to our means and purposes.
So too with strangeness not to be ignored,

Total eclipse or snow upon the rose,
And so with that most rare conception, nothing.
What is it, after all, but something missed?
It is the water of a dried-up well
Gone to assail the cliffs of Labrador.
There is what galled the arch-negator, sprung
From Hell to probe with intellectual sight
The cells and heavens of a given world
Which he could take but as another prison:
Small wonder that, pretending not to be,
He drifted through the bar-like boles of Eden
In a *black mist low creeping,* dragging down
And darkening with moody self-absorption
What, when he left it, lifted and, if seen
From the sun's vantage, seethed with vaulting hues.
Closer to making than the deftest fraud
Is seeing how the catbird's tail was made
To counterpoise, on the mock-orange spray,
Its light, up-tilted spine; or, lighter still,
How the shucked tunic of an onion, brushed
To one side on a backlit chopping-board
And rocked by trifling currents, prints and prints
Its bright, ribbed shadow like a flapping sail.
Odd that a thing is most itself when likened:
The eye mists over, basil hints of clove,
The river glazes toward the dam and spills
To the drubbed rocks below its crashing cullet,
And in the barnyard near the sawdust-pile
Some great thing is tormented. Either it is
A tarp torn loose and in the groaning wind
Now puffed, now flattened, or a hip-shot beast
Which tries again, and once again, to rise.
What, though for pain there is no other word,
Finds pleasure in the cruellest simile?
It is something in us like the catbird's song
From neighbor bushes in the grey of morning

That, harsh or sweet, and of its own accord,
Proclaims its many kin. It is a chant
Of the first springs, and it is tributary
To the great lies told with the eyes half-shut
That have the truth in view: the tale of Chiron
Who, with sage head, wild heart, and planted hoof
Instructed brute Achilles in the lyre,
Or of the garden where we first mislaid
Simplicity of wish and will, forgetting
Out of what cognate splendor all things came
To take their scattering names; and nonetheless
That matter of a baggage-train surprised
By a few Gascons in the Pyrenees
Which, having worked three centuries and more
In the dark caves of France, poured out at last
The blood of Roland, who to Charles his king
And to the dove that hatched the dove-tailed world
Was faithful unto death, and shamed the Devil.

 TRANSIT

A woman I have never seen before
Steps from the darkness of her town-house door
At just that crux of time when she is made
So beautiful that she or time must fade.

What use to claim that as she tugs her gloves
A phantom heraldry of all the loves
Blares from the lintel? That the staggered sun
Forgets, in his confusion, how to run?

Still, nothing changes as her perfect feet
Click down the walk that issues in the street,
Leaving the stations of her body there
As a whip maps the countries of the air.

❦ THE CATCH

From the dress-box's plashing tis-
Sue paper she pulls out her prize,
Dangling it to one side before my eyes
Like a weird sort of fish

That she has somehow hooked and gaffed
And on the dock-end holds in air —
Limp, corrugated, lank, a catch too rare
Not to be photographed.

I, in my chair, make shift to say
Some bright, discerning thing, and fail,
Proving once more the blindness of the male.
Annoyed, she stalks away

And then is back in half a minute,
Consulting, now, not me at all
But the long mirror, mirror on the wall.
The dress, now that she's in it,

Has changed appreciably, and gains
By lacy shoes, a light perfume
Whose subtle field electrifies the room,
And two slim golden chains.

With a fierce frown and hard-pursed lips
She twists a little on her stem
To test the even swirling of the hem,
Smooths down the waist and hips,

Plucks at the shoulder-straps a bit,
Then turns around and looks behind,
Her face transfigured now by peace of mind.
There is no question — it

Is wholly charming, it is she,
    As I belatedly remark,
And may be hung now in the fragrant dark
    Of her soft armory.

Biographical Notes

FLEUR ADCOCK   Born in 1934 in Papakuna, New Zealand, Fleur Adcock has lived in England since 1963. She was educated at Victoria University in Wellington, and has worked as a librarian. Her publications include *Selected Poems* (1983) and *The Incident Book* (1986), published by Oxford University Press.

ELIZABETH BISHOP   Born in 1911 in Worcester, Massachusetts, Elizabeth Bishop was educated at Vassar. Her *Complete Poems 1927–1979* was published by Farrar, Straus and Giroux in 1979. Elizabeth Bishop died the same year.

MICHAEL BLUMENTHAL   Born in 1949 in Vineland, New Jersey, Mr. Blumenthal was educated at the State University of New York at Binghamton and Cornell Law School. He has worked as a television producer, speech writer, editor, and teacher. His books include *Against Romance* (Viking Penguin, 1987).

ALISON BRACKENBURY   Born in 1953 in Gainsborough, Lincolnshire, Alison Brackenbury was educated at Oxford. She has worked as a librarian. Her books include *Dreams of Power* (1981) and *Breaking Ground* (1984), published by Carcanet.

STANLEY BURNSHAW   Born in 1906 in New York City, Mr. Burnshaw was educated at the University of Pittsburgh and Cornell. He was founder of The Dryden Press and vice president of Holt, Rinehart and Winston. His books include *In the Terrified Radiance* (George Braziller, 1972) and *Mirages: Travel Notes in the Promised Land* (Doubleday, 1977).

HENRI COLE   Born in 1956 in Fukuoka, Japan, Mr. Cole grew

up in Virginia and was educated at the College of William and Mary, the University of Wisconsin, and Columbia. He lives in New York City. He is the author of *The Marble Queen* (Atheneum, 1986).

HENRI COULETTE Born in 1927 in Los Angeles, Mr. Coulette was educated at Los Angeles State College and the University of Iowa. Mr. Coulette died in 1988. His books include *The Family Goldschmidtt* (Scribner's, 1972).

DONALD DAVIE Born in 1922 in Barnsley, Yorkshire, Mr. Davie was educated at Cambridge. He has taught at Stanford and Vanderbilt. His books include *Collected Poems 1970–1983* (1983), published by Carcanet in England and by Notre Dame in the United States.

DICK DAVIS Born in 1945 in Portsmouth, Hampshire, Mr. Davis was educated at Cambridge University. He has taught at the University of California at Santa Barbara. His books include *Seeing the World* (1980) and *The Covenant* (1984), published by Anvil.

PETER DAVISON Born in 1928 in New York City, Mr. Davison was educated at Harvard and Cambridge. He has had a long career in publishing. His books include *Praying Wrong: New and Selected Poems, 1957–1984* (Atheneum, 1984).

PETER KANE DUFAULT Born in 1923 in Newark, New Jersey, Mr. Dufault was educated at Harvard. He was a bomber pilot during World War II. He is a bagpiper, fiddler, dance caller, and professional soccer official. His books include *On Balance: Selected Poems* (Sagarin, 1978).

DOUGLAS DUNN Born in 1942 in Inchinnan, Renfrewshire, Scotland, Mr. Dunn was educated at the University of Hull. He has worked as a librarian. His books include *Elegies* (1985) and *Selected Poems 1964–1983* (1986), published by Faber and Faber.

CHARLES EDWARD EATON Born in 1919 in Winston-Salem, North Carolina, Mr. Eaton was educated at the University of North Carolina, Princeton, and Harvard. He is a former vice consul at the American Embassy in Rio de Janeiro. His publications include *New and Selected Poems: 1942–1987* (Cornwall, 1987).

DANIEL MARK EPSTEIN   Born in 1948 in Washington, D.C., Mr. Epstein was educated at Kenyon College. He is currently writer-in-residence at Towson State in Baltimore. His books include *Book of Fortune* (1979) and *Spirits* (1987), published by Overlook.

JAMES FENTON   Born in 1949 in Lincoln, Lincolnshire, Mr. Fenton was educated at Oxford. He has been a political journalist, foreign correspondent, and theater reviewer. His book *The Memory of War and Children in Exile* (Penguin, 1983) was published by Random House in 1984 under the title *Children in Exile.*

DAVID FERRY   Born in 1924 in Orange, New Jersey, Mr. Ferry was educated at Amherst and Harvard. He currently teaches at Wellesley. His books include *On the Way to the Island* (Wesleyan, 1960) and *Strangers* (1983), published by the University of Chicago Press.

JOHN FULLER   Born in 1937 in Ashford, Kent, Mr. Fuller was educated at Oxford. He is currently a Fellow of Magdalen College, Oxford. His books include *Selected Poems 1954–1982* (1985), published by Secker & Warburg.

REGINALD GIBBONS   Born in 1947 in Houston, Mr. Gibbons was educated at Princeton and Stanford. He is editor of the journal *TriQuarterly.* His books include *The Ruined Motel* (Houghton Mifflin, 1981) and *Saints* (Persea, 1986).

DANA GIOIA   Born in 1950 in Los Angeles, Mr. Gioia was educated at Stanford. He currently works as an executive for a major corporation. He is the author of *Daily Horoscope* (Graywolf, 1986).

MELISSA GREEN   Born in 1954 in Boston, Melissa Green was educated at the University of Iowa and Boston University. She lives in Winthrop, Massachusetts. She is the author of *The Squanicook Eclogues* (Norton, 1987).

MARILYN HACKER   Born in 1942 in the Bronx, Marilyn Hacker was educated at New York University. She currently edits the journal *13th Moon*. Her books include *Assumptions* (Knopf, 1985) and *Love, Death, and the Changing of the Seasons* (Arbor House, 1986).

DONALD HALL   Born in 1928 in New Haven, Mr. Hall was educated at Harvard and Oxford. He taught for many years at the University of Michigan. His books include *Kicking the Leaves* (Harper & Row, 1978, and Secker & Warburg, 1979) and *The Happy Man* (Random House, 1986).

TONY HARRISON   Born in 1937 in Leeds, Yorkshire, Mr. Harrison was educated at the University of Leeds. He has taught in Nigeria and Prague, and has been resident dramatist at the National Theatre, London. His books include *Selected Poems* (Penguin, 1984, and Random House, 1987).

SEAMUS HEANEY   Born in 1939 in Castledawson, County Derry, Northern Ireland, Mr. Heaney was educated at Queen's University. He currently teaches at Harvard. His books include *Station Island* (1984) and *The Haw Lantern* (1987), published by Faber and Faber in London and by Farrar, Straus and Giroux in New York.

ANTHONY HECHT   Born in 1923 in New York City, Mr. Hecht was educated at Bard College and Columbia. He has taught at the University of Rochester. His books include *Millions of Strange Shadows* (1977) and *The Venetian Vespers* (1979), published by Atheneum in the United States and by Oxford University Press in England.

GEOFFREY HILL   Born in 1932 in Bromsgrove, Worcestershire, Mr. Hill was educated at Oxford. He currently teaches at Cambridge. His books include *Tenebrae* (André Deutsch, 1978) and *Collected Poems* (Penguin, 1985, and Oxford, 1986).

EDWARD HIRSCH   Born in 1950 in Chicago, Mr. Hirsch was educated at Grinnell and the University of Pennsylvania. He currently teaches at the University of Houston. He is the author of *For the Sleepwalkers* (1981) and *Wild Gratitude* (1986), published by Knopf.

JOHN HOLLANDER   Born in 1929 in New York City, Mr. Hollander was educated at Columbia and Indiana universities.

He now teaches at Yale. His books include *Spectral Emanations: New and Selected Poems* (Atheneum, 1976).

RICHARD HOWARD Born in 1929 in Cleveland, Mr. Howard was educated at Columbia and the Sorbonne. His translations of French literature have been published widely. His books include *Misgivings* (1979) and *Lining Up* (1984), published by Atheneum.

ANDREW HUDGINS Born in 1951 in Killeen, Texas, and raised in Montgomery, Alabama, Mr. Hudgins was educated at Huntingdon College and at Alabama, Syracuse, Iowa, and Stanford. He currently teaches at the University of Cincinnati. His books include *After the Lost War* (1987), published by Houghton Mifflin.

DONALD JUSTICE Born in 1925 in Miami, Mr. Justice was educated at the University of Miami and at Stanford. He currently teaches at the University of Florida. His books include *Selected Poems* (Atheneum, 1979, and Anvil, 1980) and *The Sunset Maker* (Atheneum, 1987).

X. J. KENNEDY Born in 1929 in Dover, New Jersey, Mr. Kennedy was educated at Seton Hall, Columbia, and the Sorbonne. He currently works as a free-lance writer. His publications include *Cross Ties: Selected Poems* (University of Georgia Press, 1985).

RICHARD KENNEY Born in 1948 in Glens Falls, New York, Mr. Kenney was educated at Dartmouth College. He currently teaches at the University of Washington. He is the author of *The Evolution of the Flightless Bird* (Yale, 1984) and *Orrery* (Atheneum, 1985).

STANLEY KUNITZ Born in 1905 in Worcester, Massachusetts, Mr. Kunitz was educated at Harvard. He has taught at numerous colleges and universities in this country and abroad. His many books include *Next-to-Last Things: New Poems and Essays* (Atlantic Monthly Press, 1985).

BRAD LEITHAUSER Born in 1953 in Detroit, Mr. Leithauser was educated at Harvard College and Harvard Law School. He was a research fellow at Kyoto Comparative Law Center from 1980 to 1983. His books include *Hundreds of Fire-*

flies (1982) and *Cats of the Temple* (1986), published by Knopf.

WILLIAM LOGAN Born in 1950 in Boston, Mr. Logan was educated at Yale and the University of Iowa. He currently teaches at the University of Florida. His books include *Difficulty* (1985) and *Sullen Weedy Lakes* (1988), published by David R. Godine.

DEREK MAHON Born in 1941 in Belfast, Mr. Mahon was educated at Trinity College, Dublin. He has been drama critic and poetry editor of *The New Statesman*. His books include *Poems 1962–1978* (1979) and *The Hunt by Night* (1982), published by Oxford University Press in England and by Wake Forest in the United States.

J. D. MCCLATCHY Born in 1945 in Bryn Mawr, Pennsylvania, Mr. McClatchy was educated at Georgetown and Yale. He has taught at Yale and Princeton, and is currently poetry editor of *The Yale Review*. He is the author of *Scenes from Another Life* (George Braziller, 1981) and *Stars Principal* (Macmillan, 1986).

JAMES MERRILL Born in 1926 in New York City, Mr. Merrill was educated at Amherst. His publications include *From the First Nine: Poems 1947–1976* (Atheneum, 1982) and *Late Settings* (Atheneum, 1985).

JAMES MICHIE Born in 1927 in Weybridge, Surrey, Mr. Michie was educated at Oxford. He currently works as editorial director of The Bodley Head. His books include *New and Selected Poems* (Chatto & Windus, 1983).

RICHARD MOORE Born in 1927 in Greenwich, Connecticut, Mr. Moore was educated at Yale University. He was formerly on the faculty of the New England Conservatory of Music. His books include *A Question of Survival* (University of Georgia Press, 1971).

FREDERICK MORGAN Born in 1922 in New York City, Mr. Morgan was educated at Princeton University. He has been editor of *The Hudson Review* since 1947. His publications include *Poems: New and Selected* (University of Illinois Press, 1987).

HERBERT MORRIS   Born in 1928 in New York City, Mr. Morris was educated at Yale and Columbia. He is a full-time writer. His books include *Peru* (1984) and *Dream Palace* (1986), published by Harper & Row.

HOWARD MOSS   1922–1987. Born in New York City, Mr. Moss was educated at Michigan, Wisconsin, and Harvard. He was, from 1947 until his death, poetry editor of *The New-Yorker*. His books include *New Selected Poems* (Atheneum, 1985).

ANDREW MOTION   Born in 1952 in London, Mr. Motion was educated at Oxford. He is the editorial director of Chatto & Windus. His books include *Dangerous Play: Poems 1974–1984* (Penguin, 1985).

PAUL MULDOON   Born in 1951 in County Armagh, Northern Ireland, Mr. Muldoon was educated at Queen's University, Belfast. He has worked as a radio and television producer. His work includes *Quoof* (1983) and *Meeting the British* (1987), published by Faber and Faber in London and by Wake Forest in the United States.

LES A. MURRAY   Born in 1938 in Nabaic, New South Wales, Australia, Mr. Murray was educated at the University of Sydney. He has been co-editor of *Poetry Australia*. His books include *The Vernacular Republic: Poems 1961–1981*, published in 1982 by Angus and Robertson in Australia and by Persea in the United States.

HOWARD NEMEROV   Born in 1920 in New York City, Mr. Nemerov was educated at Harvard College. He currently teaches at Washington University. His books include *The Collected Poems of Howard Nemerov* (1977) and *War Stories* (1987), published by the University of Chicago Press.

JOHN FREDERICK NIMS   Born in 1913 in Muskegon, Michigan, Mr. Nims was educated at the Universities of Notre Dame and Chicago. He was editor of *Poetry* (Chicago) from 1978 to 1984. His books include *The Kiss: A Jambalaya* (Houghton Mifflin, 1982).

LESLIE NORRIS   Born in 1921 in Merthyr Tydfil, Mid Glamorgan, Wales, Mr. Norris was educated at the University of

Southampton. He currently teaches at Brigham Young University. His publications include *Selected Poems* (Poetry Wales Press, 1986, Dufour Editions, 1987).

ROBERT PINSKY Born in 1940 in Long Branch, New Jersey, Mr. Pinsky was educated at Rutgers and Stanford. He currently teaches at the University of California at Berkeley. His books include *An Explanation of America* (Princeton, 1979) and *History of My Heart* (Ecco, 1984).

KATHA POLLITT Born in 1949 in New York City, Katha Pollitt was educated at Harvard and Columbia. She has been the literary editor of *The Nation*. She is the author of *Antarctic Traveller* (Knopf, 1982).

CHRISTOPHER REID Born in 1949 in Hong Kong, Mr. Reid was educated at Oxford. He has been poetry editor at Faber and Faber. His books include *Arcadia* (1979) and *Pea Soup* (1982), published by Oxford University Press.

MICHAEL J. ROSEN Born in 1954 in Columbus, Ohio, Mr. Rosen was educated at Ohio State and Columbia. He works as the literary director of The Thurber House in Columbus. He is the author of *A Drink at the Mirage* (Princeton, 1984).

GIBBONS RUARK Born in 1941 in Raleigh, North Carolina, Mr. Ruark was educated at the Universities of North Carolina and Massachusetts. He currently teaches at the University of Delaware. He is the author of *Keeping Company* (The Johns Hopkins University Press, 1983).

CAROL RUMENS Born in 1944 in London, Carol Rumens was educated at the University of London. She has worked as an advertising copywriter. Her books include *Selected Poems* (1986), published by Chatto & Windus.

MARY JO SALTER Born in 1954 in Grand Rapids, Michigan, Mary Jo Salter was educated at Harvard and Cambridge. She has taught at Harvard and Mount Holyoke. She is the author of *Henry Purcell in Japan* (Knopf, 1985).

GJERTRUD SCHNACKENBERG Born in 1953 in Tacoma, Washington, Gjertrud Schnackenberg was educated at Mount Holyoke. She is the author of *Portraits and Elegies* (Godine,

1982) and *The Lamplit Answer* (Farrar, Straus and Giroux, 1985).

ALAN SHAPIRO Born in 1952 in Boston, Mr. Shapiro was educated at Brandeis. He has taught at Northwestern. His books include *The Courtesy* (1983) and *Happy Hour* (1987), published by the University of Chicago Press.

L. E. SISSMAN Born in 1928 in Detroit, Mr. Sissman was educated at Harvard. He had a long career in advertising. His books include *Hello, Darkness: The Collected Poems of L. E. Sissman,* published in 1978 by Atlantic–Little, Brown in the United States and by Secker & Warburg in England. L. E. Sissman died in 1978.

C. H. SISSON Born in 1914 in Bristol, Mr. Sisson was educated at the Universities of Bristol, Berlin, Freiberg, and Paris. He has worked in the Ministry of Labour and as assistant under-secretary of state. His books include *Collected Poems 1943–1983* (Carcanet, 1984).

WILLIAM JAY SMITH Born in 1918 in Winnfield, Louisiana, Mr. Smith was educated at Washington, Columbia, and Oxford. He has been a Democratic member of the Vermont House of Representatives. His books include *The Traveler's Tree,* published in 1980 by Persea in the United States and in 1981 by Carcanet in England.

W. D. SNODGRASS Born in 1926 in Wilkinsburg, Pennsylvania, Mr. Snodgrass was educated at Geneva College and the State University of Iowa. He currently teaches at the University of Delaware. His books include *Selected Poems 1957–1987* (Soho Press, 1987).

ELIZABETH SPIRES Born in 1952 in Lancaster, Ohio, Elizabeth Spires was educated at Vassar College and The Johns Hopkins University. Her publications include *Globe* (Wesleyan University Press, 1981) and *Swan's Island* (Holt, Rinehart and Winston, 1985).

TIMOTHY STEELE Born in 1948 in Burlington, Vermont, Mr. Steele was educated at Stanford and Brandeis. He currently teaches at California State University at Los Angeles. He is the author of *Sapphics Against Anger and Other Poems* (Random House, 1986).

ANNE STEVENSON Born in 1933 in Cambridge, England, Anne Stevenson was educated at the University of Michigan. She has worked as a teacher and bookseller. Her books include *The Fiction-Makers* (1982) and *Selected Poems 1956–1986* (1987), published by Oxford University Press.

MAY SWENSON Born in 1919 in Logan, Utah, May Swenson was educated at Utah State University at Logan. Her publications include *New and Selected Things Taking Place* (Atlantic–Little, Brown, 1978) and *In Other Words* (Knopf, 1987).

ANTHONY THWAITE Born in 1930 in Chester, Cheshire, Mr. Thwaite was educated at Oxford University. He has worked as an editor of *The New Statesman* and *Encounter*. His publications include *A Portion for Foxes* (Oxford, 1977) and *Poems 1953–1983* (Secker & Warburg, 1984).

CHARLES TOMLINSON Born in 1927 in Stoke-on-Trent, Staffordshire, Mr. Tomlinson was educated at Cambridge. He currently teaches at the University of Bristol. His books include *The Flood* (Oxford, 1981) and *Collected Poems* (Oxford, 1985).

DAVID WAGONER Born in 1926 in Massilon, Ohio, Mr. Wagoner was educated at Pennsylvania State and Indiana. He currently teaches at the University of Washington. His books include *Through the Forest: New and Selected Poems 1977–1987* (Atlantic Monthly Press, 1987).

JEFFREY WAINWRIGHT Born in 1944 in Stoke-on-Trent, Staffordshire, Mr. Wainwright was educated at the University of Leeds. He currently teaches at Manchester Polytechnic. His books include *Heart's Desire* (1978) and *Selected Poems* (1985), published by Carcanet.

DEREK WALCOTT Born in 1930 in St. Lucia, the West Indies, Mr. Walcott was educated at the University of the West Indies. He currently teaches at Boston University. His books include *Collected Poems 1948–1984* (Farrar, Straus and Giroux, 1986).

ROBERT PENN WARREN Born in 1905 in Guthrie, Kentucky, Mr. Warren was educated at Vanderbilt, Yale, and Oxford. He is a professor emeritus at Yale. His books include *New and Selected Poems 1925–1985*, published in 1985 by Random House in New York and by Secker & Warburg in London.

ROSANNA WARREN Born in 1954 in Fairfield, Connecticut, Rosanna Warren was educated at Yale and Johns Hopkins. She currently teaches at Boston University. She is the author of *Each Leaf Shines Separate* (Norton, 1984).

THEODORE WEISS Born in 1916 in Reading, Pennsylvania, Mr. Weiss was educated at Muhlenberg College and Columbia University. He was the founding editor of the *Quarterly Review of Literature*. His books include *From Princeton One Autumn Afternoon* (Macmillan, 1987).

RICHARD WILBUR Born in 1921 in New York City, Mr. Wilbur was educated at Amherst. He currently teaches at Smith. His books include *The Mind-Reader* (1977) and *New and Collected Poems* (1988), both published by Harcourt Brace Jovanovich.

Acknowledgments

FLEUR ADCOCK. "Future Work," "A Message," and "Weathering" are from *Selected Poems*. Copyright © 1983 by Fleur Adcock. Reprinted by permission of Oxford University Press.

ELIZABETH BISHOP. "The Moose" and "One Art" are from *The Complete Poems 1927–1979*. Copyright © 1983 by Alice Helen Methfessel. Copyright © 1975, 1976 by Elizabeth Bishop. Reprinted by permission of Farrar, Straus and Giroux.

MICHAEL BLUMENTHAL. "Inventors" is from *Sympathetic Magic*. Copyright © 1980 by Michael Blumenthal. Reprinted by permission of the author.

ALISON BRACKENBURY. "Whose Window?" and "The Divers' Death" are from *Dreams of Power and Other Poems*. Copyright © 1978 by Alison Brackenbury. Reprinted by permission of Carcanet Press.

STANLEY BURNSHAW. "Talmudist" is from *Mirages: Travel Notes in the Promised Land*. Copyright © 1977 by Stanley Burnshaw. Reprinted by permission of the author.

HENRI COLE. "The Prince Enters the Forest" is from *The Marble Queen*. Copyright © 1986 by Henri Cole. Reprinted by permission of Atheneum Publishers, an imprint of Macmillan.

HENRI COULETTE. "Postscript" and "Correspondence" are from the January 1985 issue of *The New Criterion*. Reprinted by permission of the author.

DONALD DAVIE. "Rousseau in His Day" and "Ox-Bow" are from *Collected Poems 1970–1983*. Copyright © 1983 by Donald Davie. Reprinted by permission of Carcanet Press.

DICK DAVIS. "Childhood of a Spy" is from *The Covenant*. Copyright © 1984 by Dick Davis. Reprinted by permission of Anvil Press Poetry.

PETER DAVISON. "The Vanishing Point" and "Questions of Swimming, 1935" are from *Praying Wrong: New and Selected Poems 1957–1984*. Copyright © 1984 by Peter Davison. Reprinted by permission of Atheneum Publishers, an imprint of Macmillan.

PETER KANE DUFAULT. "A First Night" first appeared in *The Poetry Pilot*. Copyright © 1986 by Peter Kane Dufault. Reprinted by permission of the author.

DOUGLAS DUNN. "Elegy for the Lost Parish" is from *Barbarians*. Copyright © 1979 by Douglas Dunn. Reprinted by permission of Faber and Faber. "War Blinded" is from *St. Kilda's Parliament*. Copyright © 1981 by Douglas Dunn. Reprinted by permission of Faber and Faber.

ACKNOWLEDGMENTS

CHARLES EDWARD EATON. "The Lynx" is from the January 1987 issue of *The New Criterion*. Reprinted by permission of the author.

DANIEL MARK EPSTEIN. "The Barrel Organ" and "Old Times" are from *Spirits*. Copyright © 1987 by Daniel Mark Epstein. Reprinted by permission of The Overlook Press.

JAMES FENTON. "God, A Poem" is from *Children in Exile: Poems 1968–1984*. Copyright © 1983 by James Fenton. Reprinted by permission of Sterling Lord Literistic and the author.

DAVID FERRY. "Cythera" and "Rereading Old Writing" are from *Strangers*. Copyright © 1983 The University of Chicago. Reprinted by permission of The University of Chicago Press.

JOHN FULLER. "Sonata" and "St. Sophia" are from *Selected Poems 1954–1982*. Copyright © 1985 by John Fuller. Reprinted by permission of Secker & Warburg.

REGINALD GIBBONS. "Hoppy" is from *The Ruined Motel*. Copyright © 1981 by Reginald Gibbons. Reprinted by permission of Houghton Mifflin Company.

DANA GIOIA. "California Hills in August" is from *Daily Horoscope*. Copyright © 1986 by Dana Gioia. Reprinted by permission of Graywolf Press. "The Next Poem" first appeared in *Poetry*. Copyright © 1985 by Dana Gioia. Reprinted by permission of the author.

MELISSA GREEN. "The Squanicook Eclogues: October, ii," is from *The Squanicook Eclogues*. Copyright © 1987 by Melissa Green. Reprinted by permission of W. W. Norton.

MARILYN HACKER. "Imaginary Translation" is from *Separations*. Copyright © 1975 by Marilyn Hacker. Reprinted by permission of Alfred A. Knopf.

DONALD HALL. "O Cheese" is from *Kicking the Leaves*. Copyright © 1978 by Donald Hall. Reprinted by permission of Harper & Row and the author. "Granite and Grass" is from *The Happy Man*. Copyright © 1986 by Donald Hall. Reprinted by permission of Random House and the author.

TONY HARRISON. "Book Ends I," "Confessional Poetry," and "The Queen's English" are from *Selected Poems*. Copyright © 1984, 1985 by Tony Harrison. Reprinted by permission of the author.

SEAMUS HEANEY. "A Peacock's Feather" is from *The Haw Lantern*. Copyright © 1987 by Seamus Heaney. Reprinted by permission of Farrar, Straus and Giroux and Faber and Faber Ltd.

ANTHONY HECHT. "The Deodand" is from *The Venetian Vespers*. Copyright © 1979 by Anthony Hecht. Reprinted by permission of Atheneum Publishers, an imprint of Macmillan. "The Ghost in the Martini" is from *Millions of Strange Shadows*. Copyright © 1977 by Anthony Hecht. Reprinted by permission of Atheneum Publishers, an imprint of Macmillan.

GEOFFREY HILL. "Veni Coronaberis," the section from "The Mystery of the Charity of Charles Péguy," and the poem from "Hymns to Our Lady of Chartres" are from *Collected Poems*. Copyright © 1985 by Geoffrey Hill. Reprinted by permission of Oxford University Press and André Deutsch Ltd.

EDWARD HIRSCH. "Fast Break" is from *Wild Gratitude*. Copyright © 1985 by Edward Hirsch. Reprinted by permission of Alfred A. Knopf.

JOHN HOLLANDER. "The Old Guitar" is from *Blue Wine*. Copyright © 1979 by John Hollander. Reprinted by permission of The Johns Hopkins University Press.

RICHARD HOWARD. The excerpt from "Ithaca: The Palace at Four A.M." is from *Lining Up*. Copyright © 1984 by Richard Howard. Reprinted by permission of Atheneum Publishers, an imprint of Macmillan.

ANDREW HUDGINS. "The Persistence of Nature in Our Lives" is from *Saints and Strangers*. Copyright © 1985 by Andrew Hudgins. Reprinted by permission of Houghton Mifflin Company.

DONALD JUSTICE. "Children Walking Home from School Through Good Neighborhood," "Psalm and Lament," and "In Memory of the Unknown Poet, Robert Boardman Vaughn" are from *The Sunset Maker*. Copyright © 1987 by Donald Justice. Reprinted by permission of Atheneum Publishers, an imprint of Macmillan.

X. J. KENNEDY. "Hangover Mass" is from *Cross Ties: Selected Poems*. Copyright © 1985 by X. J. Kennedy. Reprinted by permission of the author and The University of Georgia Press. "Terse Elegy for J. V. Cunningham" was first published in the October 1985 issue of *The New Criterion*. Copyright © 1985 by X. J. Kennedy. Reprinted by permission of the author.

RICHARD KENNEY. "La Brea" is from *The Evolution of the Flightless Bird*. Copyright © 1984 by Richard Kenney. Reprinted by permission of Yale University Press.

STANLEY KUNITZ. "The Wellfleet Whale" is from *Next-to-Last Things: New Poems and Essays*. Copyright © 1985 by Stanley Kunitz. Reprinted by permission of Atlantic Monthly Press.

BRAD LEITHAUSER. "Angel" is from *Hundreds of Fireflies*. Copyright © 1980 by Brad Leithauser. "The Tigers of Nanzen-ji" is from *Cats of the Temple*. Copyright © 1985 by Brad Leithauser. Both are reprinted by permission of Alfred A. Knopf.

WILLIAM LOGAN. "Moorhen" is from *Moorhen and Other Poems*. Copyright © 1984 by William Logan. Reprinted by permission of the author. "Moorhen" first appeared in *Grand Street*.

DEREK MAHON. "Table Talk" and "A Garage in Co. Cork" are from *The Hunt by Night*. Copyright © 1982 by Derek Mahon. Reprinted by permission of Oxford University Press.

J. D. MCCLATCHY. "At a Reading" is from *Stars Principal*. Copyright ©.1985 by J. D. McClatchy. Reprinted by permission of Macmillan.

JAMES MERRILL. "Losing the Marbles" first appeared in *The New Yorker*. Copyright © 1986 by James Merrill. Reprinted by permission of the author.

JAMES MICHIE. "Nine Times" and "Discoverer" are from *New and Selected Poems*. Copyright © 1983 by James Michie. Reprinted by permission of the author.

RICHARD MOORE. "The Visitors" first appeared in the winter 1979 issue of *The Southern Review*. Reprinted by permission of the author.

FREDERICK MORGAN. "February 11, 1977" is from *Poems New and Selected*. Copyright © 1987 by Frederick Morgan. Reprinted by permission of the author and the University of Illinois Press.

HERBERT MORRIS. "The Road" is from *Peru*. Copyright © 1983 by Herbert Morris. Reprinted by permission of Harper & Row.

HOWARD MOSS. "Morning Glory" is from *New Selected Poems*. Copyright

© 1985 by Howard Moss. Reprinted by permission of Atheneum Publishers, an imprint of Macmillan.

ANDREW MOTION. "Writing" and "These Days" are from *Dangerous Play: Poems 1974–1984* (Penguin, 1985). Copyright © 1984 by Andrew Motion. Reprinted by permission of the author.

PAUL MULDOON. "Why Brownlee Left" is from *Why Brownlee Left*. Copyright © 1980 by Paul Muldoon. Reprinted by permission of Wake Forest University Press and Faber and Faber Ltd.

LES A. MURRAY. "The Widower in the Country" and "Sydney and the Bush" are from *The Vernacular Republic: Selected Poems*. Copyright © 1982 by Les A. Murray. Reprinted by permission of Persea Books and Angus and Robertson Publishers.

HOWARD NEMEROV. "Insomnia I" and "The Makers" are from *Sentences*. Copyright © 1980 by Howard Nemerov. "The War in the Air" is from *War Stories*. Copyright © 1987 by Howard Nemerov. All of the poems are reprinted by permission of the author.

JOHN FREDERICK NIMS. "Tide Turning" is from *The Kiss: A Jambalaya*. Copyright © 1982 by John Frederick Nims. Reprinted by permission of Houghton Mifflin Company.

LESLIE NORRIS. "The Girls of Llanbadarn — Merched Llanbadarn" is from *Selected Poems*. Copyright © 1986 by Leslie Norris. Reprinted by permission of Poetry Wales Press.

ROBERT PINSKY. "Ralegh's Prizes" is from *History of My Heart*. Copyright © 1984 by Robert Pinsky. Reprinted by permission of The Ecco Press.

KATHA POLLITT. "Of the Scythians" and "Two Fish" are from *Antarctic Traveller*. Copyright © 1981 by Katha Pollitt. Reprinted by permission of Alfred A. Knopf.

CHRISTOPHER REID. "The Gardeners" is from *Arcadia*. Copyright © 1979 by Christopher Reid. Reprinted by permission of Oxford University Press.

MICHAEL J. ROSEN. "Total Eclipse" is from *A Drink at the Mirage*. Copyright © 1984 by Princeton University Press. Reprinted by permission of Princeton University Press.

GIBBONS RUARK. "Larkin" first appeared in the January 1987 issue of *The New Criterion*. Reprinted by permission of the author.

CAROL RUMENS. "Vocation" and "In the Cloud of Unknowing" are from *Direct Dialling*. Copyright © 1985 by Carol Rumens. Reprinted by permission of the author and Chatto & Windus.

MARY JO SALTER. "England" and "Welcome to Hiroshima" are from *Henry Purcell in Japan*. Copyright © 1984 by Mary Jo Salter. Reprinted by permission of Alfred A. Knopf.

GJERTRUD SCHNACKENBERG. "Supernatural Love" is from *The Lamplit Answer*. Copyright © 1982, 1985 by Gjertrud Schnackenberg. Reprinted by permission of Farrar, Straus and Giroux and Century Hutchinson.

ALAN SHAPIRO. "Familiar Story" is from *Happy Hour*. Copyright © 1987 by The University of Chicago. Reprinted by permission of the author.

L. E. SISSMAN. "Cockaigne: A Dream" and "December 27, 1966" are from *Hello, Darkness: The Collected Poems of L. E. Sissman*. Copyright © 1978 by

Anne B. Sissman. These poems first appeared in *The New Yorker*. Reprinted by permission of Little, Brown and Company in association with Atlantic Monthly Press and Martin Secker and Warburg.

C. H. SISSON. "Black Rocks" is from *Collected Poems*. Copyright © 1984 by C. H. Sisson. Reprinted by permission of Carcanet Press.

WILLIAM JAY SMITH. "Journey to the Interior" first appeared in *Poetry*. Copyright © 1987 by William Jay Smith. Reprinted by permission of the author. "Bachelor's-Buttons" is from *The Traveler's Tree: New and Selected Poems*. Copyright © 1980 by William Jay Smith. Reprinted by permission of Persea Books and the author.

W. D. SNODGRASS. "Mutability" is from *Selected Poems 1957–1987*. Copyright © 1987 by W. D. Snodgrass. Reprinted by permission of Soho Press.

ELIZABETH SPIRES. "Two Shadows" is from *Swan's Island*. Copyright © 1985 by Elizabeth Spires. Reprinted by permission of Henry Holt and Company. "0°" is from the November 1985 issue of *The New Criterion*. Reprinted by permission of the author.

TIMOTHY STEELE. "The Sheets" is from *Sapphics Against Anger and Other Poems*. Copyright © 1986 by Timothy Steele. Reprinted by permission of Random House. "Aurora" appeared in the October 1987 issue of *The New Criterion*. Reprinted by permission of the author.

ANNE STEVENSON. "The Price," "The Fiction-Makers," and "Making Poetry" are from *Selected Poems*. Copyright © 1987 by Anne Stevenson. Reprinted by permission of Oxford University Press.

MAY SWENSON. "Morning at Point Dume" is from *In Other Words*. Copyright © 1987 by May Swenson. Reprinted by permission of Alfred A. Knopf.

ANTHONY THWAITE. "Simple Poem" and "Dream Time" are from *Poems 1953–1983*. Copyright © 1984 by Anthony Thwaite. Reprinted by permission of Curtis Brown.

CHARLES TOMLINSON. "Rhymes" and "The Shaft" are from *Collected Poems*. Copyright © 1985 by Charles Tomlinson. Reprinted by permission of Oxford University Press.

DAVID WAGONER. "My Father's Garden" and "On Motel Walls" are from *Through the Forest: New and Selected Poems, 1977–1987*. Copyright © 1987 by David Wagoner. Reprinted by permission of Atlantic Monthly Press.

JEFFREY WAINWRIGHT. "The Fierce Dream" and "Illumination" are from *Heart's Desire*. Copyright © 1978 by Jeffrey Wainwright. Reprinted by permission of Carcanet Press.

DEREK WALCOTT. "The Young Wife" is from *The Arkansas Testament*. Copyright © 1987 by Derek Walcott. Reprinted by permission of Farrar, Straus and Giroux.

ROBERT PENN WARREN. "What Voice at Moth-Hour," "History During Nocturnal Snowfall," and "Last Meeting" are from *New and Selected Poems 1923–1985*. Copyright © 1985 by Robert Penn Warren. Reprinted by permission of Random House.

ROSANNA WARREN. "History as Decoration" and "To Max Jacob" are from *Each Leaf Shines Separate*. Copyright © 1984 by Rosanna Warren. Reprinted by permission of W. W. Norton.

ACKNOWLEDGMENTS

THEODORE WEISS. "Another and Another and . . ." and the first section of "Every Second Thought" are from *From Princeton One Autumn Afternoon: Collected Poems, 1950–1986*. Copyright © 1987 by Theodore Weiss. Reprinted by permission of Macmillan.

RICHARD WILBUR. "Lying," "Transit," and "The Catch" are from *New and Collected Poems*. Copyright © 1979, 1983 by Richard Wilbur. Reprinted by permission of Harcourt Brace Jovanovich.